Crimson Purple
Emilia Sayaka Sarajlija

© 2022, Emilia Sayaka Sarajlija
Printed and published by: BoD - Books
on Demand, Norderstedt
ISBN: 978-91-8007-888-7

It is a gloomy night in a modern, parallel Tokyo. As we look down upon the big city, you would expect it to be lit up with people, even at this time. Surprisingly though, there are barely folks around. A tired-looking man in an office suit carrying papers, a drunk fellow stumbling around with his empty bottle… There are not many on the main streets indeed. Perhaps it is because of the incredibly heavy fog that has laid itself like a blanket over the areas we can see, maybe because of the obvious reason that it is very late. Or is it because of the recent potential dangers that has begun lurking behind every dark corner, unseen, unheard and unknown? With the little we have observed, we can tell that this potential danger is not a made-up illusion. A darkness no one could fathom has broken through the blanket of fog and the smell of a bittersweet, yet cruel evil is in the air. Something has arrived, but none is aware of what it exactly is. Only the humans who become victims of this abnormality can look the perpetrator in the eye and learn a fact they still cannot comprehend, as they take a painful but quick last breath and disappear from this world.

Continuing to scan, we begin to dig closer and deeper into the abyss of Tokyo's more shady squares, mostly consisting of just as shady beings, apart from small love hotels here and there. Even a love hotel has its secret though; we have not been particularly keen with looking for more signs of life, but this case seems interesting. A middle-aged man exits a love hotel hurriedly. What strikes our interest is not how he looks like, since he has a completely normal and average appearance for a man of his age. What intrigues us is his actions. A smug grin appears on his face as he stands for a moment outside the entrance door to the love hotel and pulls out jewelry and money from his pockets. He does a speedy examination of the content in his hands and pulls them back into his pockets before anyone has gotten a look at it. Unfortunately for him, someone spots him and has been hiding in the shadows ever since he came out from the little hotel. A young woman is sitting on the rooftop of a nearby building. As far from what we can see, she seems to be in her late teenage years of life. She has a petite-built shape to her body, but we can tell that she is strong nevertheless, giving her composed posture and threatening dark purple eyes that is almost trying to stare this man to death. How did she manage to get up on the building's roof to begin with?

And then, it happens: The middle-aged man, as if answering to her unspoken threats, locks eyes with the adolescent woman. His smile disappears and his brown orbs fills up with fear in an instant, and his legs start going off as fast as they can, even though he knows that they cannot carry him far.

"Time for another simple hunt, I suppose. It gets awfully boring when they make it this easy for me", the girl quietly sighs the words to herself in a beautiful but serious tone as she picks herself up, jumps down from the top of the roof and begins chasing the man in the speed of light. His rapidity is not something that seems to save him though, as she keeps standing in front of him every time he turns around a corner in the valleys. It is like she has the ability of teleportation on her side, her with her extraordinary stamina and willpower to get ahold of this man. Why is she after him though? Is it the valuables she wants, or is it his life? At the same time, why would she want to take a stranger's small worth, that is like the size of a pebble? All questions imaginable is coming and going through the middle-aged one's head as he is running out of breath and finds himself in a dumpster valley. It is a dead end. He never did pay one bit of attention to where he was letting his legs take him, but maybe this is the fate of the man to face the dark purple-eyed young lady. He does not want to accept such a fate though, even when he hastily turns around and sees her standing there, with her breath fully intact.

"Stay away from me, please! If it's the money you want, just take it!", the exhausted man pushes out those words from his lungs as he pulls out the pricey jewelry and a few thousand Yen from his light-brown coat and casts them in front of the purple-eyed. She slowly draws closer and leans down to inspect the items laying on the ground. As she gently touches a fancy pink ring, her amethyst orbs light up a bit, like a magical gem. After a couple of seconds, she throws the ring away and mumbles to herself, but loud enough for the older man to hear it.

"It is just as I suspected. He persuaded a prostitute to visit that love hotel with him… entered a room with her… pushed her around like a puppet on a string… and raped her until she couldn't breathe anymore", she mutters. And with every word, her voice becomes rawer; she is clearly angry, and the man notices it, shivering in fear and shock at the thought of what she knows and what she wants to do with him.

"How do you know— ", he tries to speak up but is interrupted by her.

"You are already admitting it? Boy, you really are an easy target to kill."

"Kill…?! No, I beg you to spare me! Listen— "

"Shut the hell up, filthy rapist", she says as she runs to the middle-aged one with her inhuman speed, uses her mere hands to bend his thin neck until it cracks and reveals her long teeth as she furiously sinks them into the flesh of her victim. The man does not even have time to scream in pain. It all happens in a second, but it is feeling like an eternity for the young lady. She continues to suck his blood, and the taste is supple and satisfying. His eyes widen, his mouth hangs open, his skin turns pale from being empty and the body drops down next to the dumpster. After she is done with her work, an even more mysterious man jumps down from a building out of nowhere and positions himself behind the adolescence.

"Clear?"

"Clear", she responds to him before the strange man and the girl jumps into the darkness of the night, leaving the lifeless body behind.

It is morning. The sun is trying its best to break through the Sakura-patterned curtains and into the bedroom, filling it with hues of a fierce red, a mild orange and a pretty pink. A girl sleeping on the top of a bunk bed is starting to slowly wake up from the sun's colors shimmering into her beautiful blue eyes, as if being her alarm clock. Her mouth lets out a quick yawn as she sits up and rubs her eyes while scanning the room. There is no doubt that this is a small home, since the room does not consist of many things, but we can also tell that this is a very girly room, considering the Sakura curtains, the white bunk bed, the idol posters on the walls… there are also two wooden tight closets next to the beds and two desks, one having books and writing material on it and the other one having makeup and CDs on it. Another girl is in the bedroom, though she is awake and sitting at one of the desks, occupied with something. Appearance-wise, she resembles the girl on the bed so much that they are most likely twins. The only distinguishable difference is their hair color: One has hazel brown hair and the other has pure black. "You're awake, Ayaka?", the girl at the desk says out loud while continuing with her business, but we can tell that she is talking to her sleepy sister, whose name is apparently Ayaka. As soon as she hears the question, she almost jumps down from the bunk bed and hurries to hug her twin firmly from behind, with a smile stretching across her fine-shaped face.

"Ayame! As always, my diligent sister is awake and sitting at her desk, doing whatever while waiting for me to wake up!", Ayaka happily says and then rests her head on Ayame's left shoulder to peek at what she is doing.

"I'm practicing poetry and calligraphy again. I find it to be such a wonderful combination. It's time-consuming but calming at the same time. You should try it sometime."

"Hmm… Nah. You're the old and traditional soul here, not me. There's no way I'd be able to draw in the gorgeous style that you do anyways, even if I try!"

"Haha, I suppose that's true. I find my soul to be kind of old too when I think about it", Ayame confirms with a small smile showing on her face as she continues to focus on the ink and paper. She seems to be the type of teenager who is often in her own world, filled with seriousness and art, while Ayaka's world is a bit more open and carefree. They may be twins, but both have strengths and weaknesses that makes them slightly different. That does not mean they don't have anything in common though.

"Considering you love the bed, you're up quite early. It is 5:06 AM, and you usually sleep until our karate lessons at 7:00 AM", Ayame states while steadily letting the brush flow and form Japanese characters.

"Of course I woke up now: I sleep more than you to make sure that I am strong enough for training and school. But this time, I had to experience the wonderful sunrise! You know I love when the sun rises, just like you enjoy watching when the sun sets", Ayaka responds brightly while opening the curtains and letting the sun kiss her lips.

After becoming more awake and warmed up, she proceeds to walk to her closet to take off her dark blue pajamas and put on a daily attire that suits her: a medium-long, simple white dress with matching white stockings patterned with red roses and leaves. After being happy with her clothing choice, she goes to sit on the desk beside Ayame's to brush her messy light brown hair and to put on a bit of a crème foundation to her face. She looks at herself in the mirror several times to make sure that she's happy with today's look and smiles when she's complete. Ayame's closet seems to have more casual clothes and darker colors though, as she is wearing merely a black pair of tight jeans and a purple T-shirt with the Japanese character for "love" written in the middle of the shirt. Each sister has their preferences and tastes, but everything about them suits just right.

"How do I look?", Ayaka asks as she stands up and makes a humorous model pose, waiting for a positive response.

"As beautiful as a blooming rosebud", Ayame answers in a serious but affectionate tone.

"You're too sweet, Ayame! And you don't have to be jealous: I can tell that you are when it comes to my appearance... but I need you to know that you are more beautiful than me. The auras that you give off apply to your beauty too! Also, remember how you are popular with both students and teachers in school for being so cool yet old-fashioned?

People look up to you and everything that you are. I mean, look at your long and straight black hair, your flawless body that any guy would want their girlfriend to have— "

"You're babbling again, Ayaka", Ayame interrupts to speak. "Besides, it actually sounds like you are the jealous one", she says with a now confident tone to her voice and a smug smile, making her sister flustered as she just caught her in a lie. They both decide to laugh it off.

"We should go eat breakfast. I'm sure everybody's in the kitchen... I also know that you're starving", Ayame proclaims with another overconfident expression.

"What makes you think I am hungry, sister? I can survive without food!", Ayaka says and, before she even has time to hide another lie, her growling stomach reveals the truth.

"Come on, silly", Ayame giggles while dragging Ayaka out of their bedroom and right into the kitchen, where they are warmly welcomed by the other family members.

"Good morning, my daughters!", mother Izumi greets happily her girls when she hears them walking out of their room. She is sitting on the floor at the square-shaped Japanese table with a very young and small child, helping him eat some crushed vegetables. Beside her and the young one, there's a man with glasses and a newspaper sitting down as well. He greets the adolescences with a firm nod and a sincere smile before he goes on with reading. Ayaka looks around and notices that someone is missing, so she asks the man for confirmation.

"Father, where is big sis?"

"Reina had an early shift at the office that she needed to take", father Yasu flatly responds while focusing so much on reading the papers that an eye wrinkle appears and goes away in the level of concentration. Izumi adds some words to the conversation.

"Your big sister is very hardworking and devoted to your father's company and that is how she got the job, even without much experience on the workplace. Reina shows great potential and I hope you two will be reminded of that, now when you are preparing for your final exams."

"Of course. We will not disappoint you or father", Ayame says with determination in her voice as she responds to the motivation their loving mother is trying to give. Yasu looks proudly at Ayame but disappointedly at Ayaka, who is not saying anything or even indicating that she is listening. She seems to worry over something, and that something could be anything.

"Anyway, you two should make some breakfast for yourselves. I would help if I could but I have to finish feeding your little brother. Sora is a hungry boy!", Izumi tells the girls, and now that the topic is food, Ayaka snaps out of her thoughts and onto the fridge... but then, she hesitates again, and whispers a few words to Ayame.

"Hey... can you cook something for me? Anything, pretty please?" Ayame looks confusingly at her twin and asks, "I thought you knew how to cook?"

"I know how to, but your food tastes amazing! Please?"

"Well, make a meal with me then. I'll teach you the ways of the culinary arts! What do you say about some okonomiyaki?", Ayame whispers back and gets a smile filled with gratitude from Ayaka in response. Their parents take a quick look at them as their daughters are happily working together to try to cook the best Japanese pancakes ever, and they feel just as happy to have raised a big yet stable family.

"It is finally done!", Ayaka announces after 30-45 minutes in a loud tone while spinning around and showing her mother and father a plate stuffed with the okonomiyaki she made with her sister.

"Have a taste and let us know what you think", Ayame adds, in her usual calm voice. Yasu's eyes broaden a bit while still reading his news articles. He is clearly surprised by something he read.

"Izumi, you taste their food. Ayame learned her cooking from you, after all", Yasu says in a monotone way, completely uninterested in engaging to the twins' effort and conversation. They take heed to their father's lack of interest because of one of the articles, and so they ask him what is wrong.

"You should read this", he flatly answers while putting the newspaper on the table and pointing at one piece of text. Ayaka comes closer to read out loud the headline.

"Latest news: Prostitute and customer found dead last night" … The twins sit there in a confusing state, as they do not seem very shocked. Yasu speaks up.

"Look at what's written about their deaths. The customer was a man in his 50s. His body was just like the other victims that's been reported. No blood in his body, yet no open wounds. His DNA was found all over the 18-year-old prostitute's body, so the police assume he beat and raped her to death, and then somehow got himself killed quickly afterwards."

"Despite everyone being used to that news these days, it is always horrible, every time this happens", Izumi suddenly says while hand-washing the dishes. "That girl was around your ages, Ayame, Ayaka". Their mother gets more emotional the more she speaks. She finishes the dishes, and by the time she turns around to face her daughters, her eyes are slightly filled with tears. "Please, my beautiful girls… be extra careful when you go outside. Don't let anything happen to you", Izumi says heartfelt while closing her eyes and hugging her daughters tightly. Yasu puts the newspaper away and decides to leave for work, mostly to look after Reina there. Before he closes the entrance door, Ayame quickly expresses herself.

"Be careful, father. None of us can afford to lose you either."

"Always careful", Yasu responds with a small but confident smile to cheer his worried daughter up and heads out into the huge city.

Yasu Nakashima is a proud and firm family businessman who moved to a part of Tokyo called Shinjuku, where administrative opportunities are better, to attempt to start his own small company and gradually build it up. Times are rough now though, with all the mysterious killings going around not only Shinjuku, but the entire Tokyo. This has been a lazy investigation without progress by the police because of everybody's fear of losing their lives. Policemen only clean up the mess, but nothing more is being done to try preventing whatever creature it is that is responsible for the murders from going further. The entire city, its people and its businesses will all literally get sucked dry if someone does not act. And, of course, these earlier consequences that has followed along with the weird deaths has also affected the Nakashima business to stay still for now, but Yasu does his best to remain hopeful and observant, for the sake of his family and company.

As Yasu enters the elevator, he sees an old neighbor and friend getting out from his apartment and walking towards the elevator as well. Yasu waits for him, holding the elevator doors open for the elder. He is moving a bit slow, clutching to a cane as his support for a steady walk.

"Yasu! It has been a while. Thank you for respecting the elderly and waiting for me and my cane", the old friend says with a friendly laughter leaving his slightly shaking mouth.

"No problem, Mr. Fukui. Indeed, it's been some time since we last hung out properly. It is always nice to see a good friend", Yasu answers with a genuine smile while clicking on an elevator button, taking them to the ground.

"Please, leave out the 'Mr.', Yasu. You know you can call me by my first name, especially after all we have been through. We are such great... 'pals', as the children usually say these days?"

"Yes, Jirou: We really are true pals", Yasu once again answers, looking at the old one so he can see the smile both has on their faces. Jirou's laughter is starting to tone down though, and his happy smile transforms into a sad one. Yasu knows exactly why that is.

"I know you miss Ichirou. It must be as heartbreaking for you as it is for me. He was my friend, and your brother." Jirou frowns at the sudden comments, reminding him of his loss.

"Trust me when I say that my grief is far bigger and deeper than yours, Yasu. Ichirou was more than a twin brother to me. Our bond was very much alike those twin daughters of yours. To have lost someone of that importance... it is like permanently losing a part of your soul. The fact that your appearance highly resembles Ichirou's makes it all worse for me."

Yasu's body fills up with an enormous guilt... knowing Jirou blames his friend for his brother's death. Yasu takes a detailed look into the earlier memories he has from his youthful days, as if trying to honor the memories they shared, while being stuck in the slowly moving elevator. What he does not exactly remember are things beyond humanity...

It is year 1997 and a tall, handsome, young man is in a dull-looking and small-sized room. His room is not particularly colorful, but gray and brown fills the space. This does not mean it's completely empty though: there are plenty of papers and books stacked up neatly on a brown desk, with a poster of the boy band SMAP taped up on the wall above the busy desk, a gray single bed is pushed into the corner of the room and a wooden wardrobe is half open, with the young adult going through it. As it is an early morning, he had just awoken and is preparing clothes to wear for the day. In the end, he chooses a light gray shirt and dark blue jeans, which he obviously does not find particularly comfortable after making a pained face, but he goes with it. After getting dressed, he looks around the room and spots a yearbook on the brown desk, laying at the edge of its seat on the brown desk. He picks it up and flips to one page that says "Yasu Nakashima" over a picture of the young Yasu holding some sort of degree in his hands and a bright smile on his face.

"Scholarship… Thank you for giving me this opportunity at this amazing university," Yasu mumbles to himself, as if starting a small prayer… but he gets interrupted by several loud knocks on his door.

"YASU, HOW LONG ARE YOU GONNA MAKE US WAIT?!", says a voice unfamiliar to us but familiar to the young one. He barely has time to open the door before two different-looking individuals storms into the small room. One is looking similar to the tired Yasu and the other one stumbles across the room as he almost falls onto the hard floor but manages to stand up properly when hitting the desk.

"What are you doing, Jirou? Behave yourself, for your own sake", the young adult standing next to Yasu says with heavy disappointment in his voice while adjusting his glasses.

"Sorry, sorry, Ichirou! But it's Yasu's damn fault for taking so long! You'll take responsibility for making us wait, won't you?", young Jirou jokes around with that well-known white smile while hugging his sleepy friend by taking his arm and letting it hang around Yasu's shoulders, being slightly pulled down by Jirou's weight.

"Come on, guys: Let me get some coffee from the dorm's kitchen, and after that, we can head out on the bicycle ride. I was up all night reading the books for next week's exam…"

"Trying to win that gal Izumi's heart, I see? You know she's Ichirou's bait, not yours," Jirou jokingly teases his friend once again. This group of three clearly has different personalities: Ichirou is the strict one and their class's student council president, Yasu is the hard-working one, including Ichirou's rival, while Jirou is the joker, purely joining university because of the fun events that comes along with it. Not to mention seeing his twin brother prestige, as he knows Ichirou would.

The three young men exits the dorm after an early cup of coffee together and ventures out into the wilderness: The campus. The place is filled with all sorts of students who has enrolled into the university for all sorts of reasons. Some may wish big future fame upon them or will be happy with just a small success. Either way, everybody has a legit motive for being here... well, everybody except Jirou. He does not seem to have any real explanation for being on the school grounds, but since the Fukui family are nowhere near a low-class family, their parents managed with ease to grant both twins' wishes of getting the same scholarship that the middle-low class family Nakashima had to work hard for to get a hold on for their only son. This school accepts both female and male students, which has made it earn its reputation as the "University of Love", as many young couples forms here and proceed to stay together for a lifetime, so there are also quite the few students that enrolls to find their true love. One young woman named Izumi Asahi is one of them: She is a first year who came to study economics and is taking the chance to kill two birds with one stone by trying to find 'the one' at campus at the same pace as her studies. Izumi is an attractive girl, with a short but strong-looking body, clear blue eyes and hazel hair that reaches down to her bottom. A different looking yet beautiful girl like that caught both Yasu's and Ichirou's eyes and hearts right away. Each of the fallen men has approached Izumi in the past, but she seems to be in a struggle when it comes to choosing who to be with, as both look similar and have honest and serious intentions. Thus, Yasu Nakashima and Ichirou Fukui became rivals, to see who will be the winner at this love race. One would expect Yasu to be jealous of his rich rival, but it is the opposite, as Ichirou feels deeply threatened. His gut feeling is telling him that he is missing that special bond, that one-of-a-kind connection, with Izumi that she has developed with Yasu. This has made Ichirou rather somber in behavior and even hateful emotions has developed inside of him... the question is, is he noticing it?

"Hey, guys!", a girly voice says loudly as she draws near the three men who just came out into the campus. Speak of the devil, it is Izumi. As soon as she is close enough, Jirou makes sure to give her a friendly hug so that she must choose herself who to hug afterwards. Jirou is obviously on his brother's side, so he feels bad for Ichirou when Izumi chooses to greet Yasu with a rather intimate hug. Ichirou frowns secretly in disgust and all sorts of negative thoughts starts going through his head, so he takes discreet action by throwing in a comment between their loving hug.

"Are you two dating? That's rather quick, don't you think?", he says while adjusting his glasses. It seems to be a habit of his to do so whenever he is feeling down in any way. Ichirou's words spoil the lovebirds' moment and gets Izumi all flustered. Noticing her light blush makes Yasu close his eyes and remember something. He smiles to himself, which pisses Ichirou off even more, but he tries to conceal his jealousy and imagines himself still having a chance. Two types of princes chasing one princess.

"Haha, Fukui-san! I'm sorry, I almost forgot to give you a hug too, but you know I would never forget you!", Izumi says while going up to him and giving the same friendly hug that she gave Jirou. Without hesitation, Ichirou embraces her and lets his nose pick up her coconut perfume while hugging her a bit too tight to feel her chest against his... Is he the nearest one to the word 'creepy' or 'desperate'? Yes. And Izumi notices this and starts feeling uncomfortable, so she tries letting go, but he holds on.

"Fukui-san... it kind of hurts," she says while looking at Yasu and Jirou, as if saying 'Help me!'.

"Oh. My apologies, Izumi. And please, do feel free to call me Ichirou. No need to be so formal," he says, totally oblivious to why she looks at him with the smallest hint of, what looks like, fear. Yasu picks up every detail from their exchange and he gets a feeling that he should be concerned regarding his lover's safety. Or maybe his rival's safety? Heck, it could be that both are in potential danger: Whatever it is that Yasu's feeling in his gut, he knows something will happen soon, but to figure out what that is, one can only wait for time to tell.

"Hey, Izumi-chan… me and the two are going for a bicycle ride in the forest. It's kinda like our 'tradition'. Care to join us?", Jirou pops up with the question from nowhere to break the awkward atmosphere.

"I would love to— but I have quite the sudden stomachache. Let's do it next time," Izumi replies while placing her hand lightly on her stomach, indicating that she is not feeling very good and not fit for an adventurous trip. Yasu looks at Izumi with an angled head and confused eyes, but after receiving a full-hearted smile from his woman, he touches his own stomach as if asking a mute question, to which she responds with a small nod. He gets into a state of shock immediately but regains his breath and posture to normal quickly enough so the guys would not notice. Now he needs to come up with a reasonable excuse to have an urgent talk with Izumi, but he can't skip out on the bicycle ride with his closest friends either, so he decides to pay Izumi a goodbye for now and go get their bikes that are sitting beside each other right around the corner. Total silence falls upon the usually chatty pair of pals as they are nearing the big parking lot that is mostly occupied by other people's bikes too and not vehicles. The lot is empty from people, making it easy for Ichirou to do something that may have been expected.

"Yasu, can we have a quick talk in private? Let us go to the corner over there."

"Sure thing," Yasu replies with a slight suspect. He knows Ichirou obviously gets rather bitter every time he sees the lovebirds cuddling up, since he passionately feels like it should be him with Izumi and not his rival. Suddenly, after turning into the corner, Ichirou pushes Yasu into the brick wall with a brute force. He has never been known to be this strong, and thus, this strength shocks Yasu. Ichirou comes closer to his victim's face and does not care to feel the need to whisper his threat:

"Take Izumi away from me and I will kill you. I can even personally execute your death to make it as painful as possible, so you can feel my suffering of seeing you get all sickeningly sweet and dear with my property."

Yasu's eyes widen and gets filled up with tears from the pain of not being able to breathe properly, since Ichirou's arm is up against Yasu's slender neck like a magnet. However, despite being in danger by his own friend's hand, a courageous Yasu tries to give a bold statement.

"Izumi is not... property..."

"Oh, really? Prove me wrong, you disgusting human."

"Human...?", Yasu spits out, confused by the usage of word. We are all humans, aren't we? But it's just when Yasu is in that thought of his that he sees a glimpse of two red orbs staring into his soul. Delusion or reality? Yasu cannot make up his dizzy mind as he feels himself slowly but surely fainting, and just as he sees white and nods off, a hero comes in: Izumi Asahi. She stands extremely confidently at the corner, with her hands resting on her waist and a furious expression covering up her normally tender face. Ichirou goes from being revengeful to surprised in a split second when he realizes that his unrequited love has heard and seen everything from the forest across the huge parking lot. But how did she hear and see from such a long distance? Ichirou gets the answers he needs as soon as she comes close enough for him to see her eyes. Her innocent sky-blue eyes have turned into an infuriated dark hue of purple. Ichirou immediately releases Yasu's body, making it drop to the ground like a lifeless corpse. Luckily enough, he is unconscious but still alive, and Izumi is thankful for that. She knows Ichirou could have killed her lover in mere seconds, considering his non-human strength that his mutated self has naturally developed since birth.

"Your purple eyes... They're beautiful, Izumi. The fact that your body has fully mutated now is extraordinary, and it's thanks to me, no? I should be rewarded with your undying love, not this weak human laying before me," Ichirou says cockily while directing his hand towards Yasu, who has no idea of the divine fact that Hell has brought out their demons into this world, and these demons have gifted specially chosen humans from birth with enormous amounts of unique powers. A human who was born with a demon soul is called Behemoth. The Fukui family have many generations being born like this, mainly because it can be genetic, despite being a power that should not be allowed into this life. Hell broke the rules, took of their chains and entered the human world.

"Why does my eyes turn purple whenever I feel this sensation? Why can I see through things? Why am I faster than ever? You haven't explained anything to me, and I NEED answers. Give me them and I won't hurt you for hurting Yasu," Izumi tells Ichirou with an angry tone to her usually melodious voice. He seems a bit cautious but makes himself ready to respond without pushing any buttons.

"As I mentioned, since you've fully mutated now, it would be foolish of me to mess with you, so I shall answer your questions."

"Mutated? Into what? What did you do to me that night you tried to rape me?"

"Take it easy. All these questions will take time to answer, you know. Besides, is it not obvious what you have become? You are a mutated form of a Behemoth. You've heard stories about them, haven't you? I know you love to read about mythology. I see you visit the library almost every day."

"Creep. Rapist. Stalker. Demon. I can think of so many horrible ways to describe you, but unfortunately, not really any good ones. Ichirou Fukui is probably not even your real name."

"No need to be rude, I am not going to harm you, my love. In fact, I am feeling ecstatic, seeing your demonic beauty finally come to life. I can think of so many wonderful ways to describe you, and fortunately, not really any bad ones. Anyway, do you want your answers or not?"

"Yes, do tell everything that you know," Izumi says sarcastically while preparing herself for more truths. The fact that she has become a form of Behemoth is brutal enough, but now she has to live with it, and thus, needs every bit of information she can get from a pure-blooded Behemoth.

"Whenever we get thirsty for blood, human or animal, our eye color changes. If you have brown eyes, they become ruby red. If you have blue eyes, they become dark purple. If you have green eyes, one iris becomes golden yellow and the other pupil becomes a dusty gray. We need to feast often and regularly so our eyes do not reveal our secret, which is partly why I made love to you."

"Raped. You did NOT make love to me: You tried to rape me, and you know it."

"Same thing, different words. Anyhow," Ichirou says coldly and continues explaining, ignoring Izumi's growling.

"You mentioned that you can see through things... that is apparently your power. You see, we all have a unique power that's specialized for pure-blooded and mutated Behemoths, and your main abilities are X-Ray vision and inhuman speed, since you also told me of how you are 'faster than ever'. Speed is something everyone gets, so it is rather common, but I have never heard of someone with X-Ray vision... you truly are astonishing," Ichirou ends the facts with a compliment that doesn't work at all on Izumi. Her mind feels like it's going to explode from all the beastly information she has gotten so far, and honestly, she doesn't want to hear any more. Except one question that is still crawling around inside her head.

"Why me?"

"Hmm? What kind of question is that, Izumi?", Ichirou asks with a smirk on his lips while he gets close enough so that he is whispering in Izumi's ear.

"... Because we are soulmates. I can't wait to spend an eternity with you, killing humans together to prove our true love in the most extreme way," he says with a soft and loving tone, then licking her earlobe, making the girl freak out in both disgust and fear.

"NO! You are not my soulmate, and I will NOT kill humans, even if I am a Behemoth! I am not you and you are not me! We will never be something special!", Izumi shrieks out, sentence after sentence, which makes Ichirou enraged. He takes a hold of her neck and brings her up into the air with a single hand as his support. His grip is strong and firm, but she decides to put her new powers to the test, so she focuses on her own hands and slides through Ichirou's body with her X-Ray vision and searches for his heart. Luckily enough for her, she does indeed go to the library a lot and has studied anatomy thoroughly, so Izumi finds his heart in no time... and crushes it with her bare hands. Ichirou loses his grip of Izumi's neck right away and falls while growing cold. His eyes quickly turn red at the brink of death, his Behemoth eye color, and Izumi double checks with her detailed vision that he really is dying. She sees his heart's arteries cut from her nails and his lungs are empty of air. One of the biggest threats to humanity, Ichirou Fukui, is finally dead. Izumi must come up with a quick plan, now that she has killed a man, knocked out his twin brother and has to heal Yasu, who still is unconscious. She decides to leave the twins' bodies where they are and leave with her lover.

When Yasu wakes up, he is in his basic room at the men's dorm. He blinks a few times and tries to regain his memories, but nothing pops up, so he wonders if everything was simply a weird dream. Then, he notices that his door is slightly open. The window is fully open to give fresh air to the dull room, so someone has been in here. Yasu does not have the energy to get up, as he feels a strange pain on parts of his neck, so he decides to wait. Maybe the person who was in here will come back? After waiting for a few minutes, Izumi calmly enters the room, holding a small-sized tray with two sandwiches and a glass of water. She puts the food on the desk and rushes to Yasu's aid as soon as she notices that he is awake. She positions herself on a wooden stool that is close to the bed; close enough to reach Yasu. He is confused as to why and how Izumi is allowed in his dorm, but makes an exception to that thought, as he is more curious to what happened to him, and so he asks a question while not knowing how complex it will be for Izumi to answer.

"What happened?"

Izumi expected this question, but she never had enough time to prepare a believable response. She doesn't want to lie, nor can she tell him the whole truth. A white lie should do it.

"Don't you remember, sweetheart? You were about to go out on a ride in the forest with your friends, but you suddenly passed out when you got to the corner of the parking lot," Izumi replied with a heartwarming smile lighting up her face to hide the dark truth underneath all that light. Yasu has known his girl for so long that he can tell Izumi is not informing him of everything. He sure is a born businessman, considering his strong intuition.

"With Ichirou and Jirou, right?"

Izumi freezes inside when she hears their names being called out so casually. What happened today was anything but casual, but she tries to remain her cool and answer his question with a truth-lie.

"About them… I… I need to tell you something, Yasu. I found them laying on the ground near you. I was almost too scared to touch their bodies, thinking they'd be dead, but I felt a pulse from Jirou. However, Ichirou… He was gone," Izumi says while tears slowly start streaming down her face. These tears are not to play with though: They are honest and true. She genuinely does regret having to kill Ichirou, but for humanity's sake, she was forced to. Including having to save Yasu and their unborn child.

"… I have no words," Yasu exclaims in a robotic voice. He seems to need time alone to sink in that not only his rival is gone, but his closest friend. How is Jirou going to feel about losing his twin brother, anyways? He tries to imagine the pain of losing someone like that, but he cannot relate, as he is an only son. Izumi decides to stay silent, filled up with all sorts of emotions over the things she's gone through at the campus today. Yasu notices her obvious tears and decides to slowly get up in a sitting position and hand out his palm towards her.

"Is it too late to tell you that everything means nothing if I can't have you?"

Izumi opens her eyes and removes her wet hands from her red face, looking straight at her love. She is surprised by the sudden change of topic, going from tragic to romantic. She is happy that he is trying to cheer both up though, and so she dries her tears.

"You're pregnant, aren't you?", Yasu says quietly, surprising Izumi once again, but only for a second. She remembers almost instantly that she had given him a hint before the three young men went their way. Yasu gathers his energy to stand up, goes to close the door and window, puts on a rather calming love song on his phone at a lower volume and stands in front of the sitting girl.

"Would you do me the honor to dance with me, Izumi?", Yasu says. He sounds nervous, so while he is closing his eyes for a few seconds, Izumi activates her purple eyes and uses her X-Ray vision to look at his heart. It's beating rapidly. That's all she needed to be informed about to know that he truly loves her, and those feelings are reciprocated. The girl nods to the boy, stands up and places her warm hand in his, uniting themselves into one being with a beautiful kiss. After a while of slow dancing, Izumi rests her head on his shoulder, but mostly as an excuse to look inside her own stomach to figure out the gender. A girl is sleeping peacefully.

"Yasu? What do you say about naming her 'Reina'?", Izumi asks softly while embracing him.

"It's a suiting name, but how do you know it's a girl?"

"I just have a gut feeling," Izumi answers while looking Yasu in the eyes, letting another kiss appear.

Yasu and Jirou finally arrive on the bottom floor, and both turn to the left to go for the apartment building's main entrance. Silence lays itself in the air between them, but then Jirou gives his friend a friendly offer.

"Would you like to join me for a bowl of ramen, Yasu? Just a quick round of some quality talk with tasty noodles so we can catch up."

"I would love to, but I cannot, unfortunately. I must go to the company's office to check on Reina. She may have intelligence in her blood, but a new job is never easy, especially when it's endless hours of sitting in a stiff chair with a computer screen full of codes, emails and such in front of you. I'm sorry," Yasu politely turns down the offer. He has isolated himself more from anything that he sees as a waste of time, like friendships and entertainment, since the younger days. Family and work are his everything, so he does not need distractions. As cold as it may sound though, he is not a heartless man. In fact, his heart is made of pure, shining gold. He has simply buried the gold a bit further within, making one misjudge him as dead serious most of the times. However, Jirou persists.

"Come on: We barely talk anymore, and that's no good! I'm sure Reina will manage. After all, she can handle herself, right? If I recall, Izumi teaches karate to all of your children."

"Well, yes... Ah, I suppose you're right. Perhaps I should loosen up a bit, especially with you, Jirou. I owe you one for trying to snap me out of the thought of business, which seems to be the only topic occupying my head", Yasu says as he admits defeat and goes outside with his friend.

They look around and, not to anyone's surprise, it is a dull day as usual, with sunlight trying its best to pierce through the heavy clouds covering the sky. It looks like drops is preparing to fall from the gray hands above, but who knows these days? It's like the weather has been affected just as much as the people from the killings. After beginning to walk to the nearest ramen stand, the clouds start to cry mildly.

"It looks like it will rain. Why don't we head back to the apartment complex and grab ourselves umbrellas?", Yasu asks while looking up to the teardrops the sky is giving off, wiping away one that has fallen onto his pale cheek.

"I don't have an umbrella since I do not mind a few drops, but if you do, I'll go to your apartment and ask Izumi for one. You can continue to walk to the ramen stand and wait for me there. I shall be back in 5 minutes," Jirou kindly suggests, and without waiting for an answer, he pats Yasu heavily on the shoulder and proceeds to turn around towards the direction of their apartments. And so, the close friends part ways.

At the cozy home of Nakashima, a doorbell suddenly rings. Izumi is watching over the little one, so her hands are busy, therefore asking Ayaka to open the door. As she slid open the door to most likely greet her father, she sees an old-looking man with a cane standing there, holding a friendly smile.

"Why hello, Ayaka! It's been so long. How are you and your mother doing?"

"Ah... excuse me, sir, but who are you?", Ayaka asks confusingly. The elder feels familiar but she still cannot quite place him in her memory that has a bad habit of either remembering something for life or not at all. Izumi peeks at the entranceway and drops everything as soon as she sees who it is. She tells her daughter to go back inside and keep Sora distracted with a children's TV show playing on the television so Izumi can take her time catching up.

"Jirou! Wow... seeing you sure brings me back to the old days! How have you been, friend?"

"Hello there, Izumi! I can tell you the same. I've been good— no, on top of the world, haha."

"I see, I see! Well, what made you come by? Do you want a cup of tea?",
Izumi kindly offers but Jirou then starts explaining the situation, how he
ran into Yasu and simply need an umbrella for the possible upcoming
rain.
"Oh, don't worry, here's an umbrella for you two. Feel free to visit
anytime, Jirou. You are always welcome," Izumi expresses her light with
another beaming smile and closes the door as Jirou starts walking.
Something does not feel right though, as she is watching her old friend
slowly but surely walk down to the hallway and into the elevator.
"What is this... uneasy feeling in my chest...?", Izumi whispers to herself,
not expecting an answer from anybody but herself.
Yasu is patiently waiting inside the ramen stand. He takes a seat and
decides to order a set of tonkotsu ramen for both him and Jirou. It has
been well over 5 minutes by now, but Yasu is not paying attention to his
watch. He tries to open a bit and starts chit-chatting with the owner of
the ramen stand. Just as he is about to pay for the pork ramen, a sudden
sensation fills him up. It feels like something is temporarily taking his
soul's place inside of his body, suffocating his own being and everything
that makes him him. He does not even have a second to think before he
is completely engulfed. His mind becomes completely dull, his skin
becomes pale white, and his eye color becomes pure black.
Yasu stands up in an awkward position, yet with no expression on his
face, and slowly begins to walk towards a specific direction. The ramen
stand owner gets both confused and angry, wondering why Yasu
changed in a snap and why he didn't pay for the meals, but since he
never began eating, the owner shrugs it off and removes the pork ramen
from the table and goes on with his own business. Yasu walks with his
head angled down, his back hunched and clumsy feet. People look at
him as if he is tipsy, making them avoid coming near him as they walk by
the strange-acting man. He eventually starts walking in a faster pace and
more normal posture, making his way towards a tall company building
with several company names written on spots of the building's walls.
One of the signs reads "Naka Accounting", which is the Nakashima's
family business' official name. It is a respected company that originated

in the Japanese city Naka, hence the choice of name. Will it hold up its reputation, especially after what the world has become?

Reina Nakashima is sitting alone in their office department, analyzing and signing papers in no hurry. She's whistling in a melodic tone as she is doing her work at her desk. Reina has grown into quite the beautiful young woman: Her shoulder-length autumn brown hair is sitting in a neat little bun on the top of her head, transparent reading glasses resting on the bridge of her nose and a grey yet sophisticated female office outfit covering up her slim body. She simply looks like a hard-working woman who loves what she does, which is not a feeling many can relate to regarding their occupations. The silence is in the air, but then it gets cut by the sound of an elevator arriving on the floor. Reina is not expecting anyone but a regular coworker, so she gets surprised when she sees her father exit the big elevator and walk towards Reina. Yasu looks completely normal, but something feels off… However, Reina brushes it off and explains to herself that it's just his "vibe".

"Good morning, father. What brings you to the office? This early too," Reina asks while greeting her father with a slight but polite bow. Her glasses fall onto her chest, making her eyesight a bit worse than usual, but manageable. Instead of answering verbally, Yasu continues to slowly walk towards Reina in the speed of a zombie and lifting his head up to show his eyes. They are completely black now and reek of death.

"Father…?", Reina says when she doesn't receive a response. She cannot see the black eyes staring into her heart, waiting for a moment to hit and strike. She quickly puts on her glasses again, seeing the horror and feeling the fear washing her mind up.

"Father!? What happened to you!? Please, snap out of it! It's me! Rei-"… The lights go out, making the current silence painful for the ears. Nothing can be seen. A thud sound, like something falling on the floor, can be heard though. If you listen closely, it sounds like something supple and meaty fell from the ceiling and down to the cold office floor. The room stinks of blood and death, if not more disturbing odors. Something (or rather, someone) was dead in mere seconds, in front of Yasu. The lights come back on, and he looks beyond horrified when he sees what he sees.

Reina. It is Reina who we heard and smelt.

CHAPTER II

The first emotion Yasu feels is a lively shock as he looks down upon the decapitated body. Her head had been cut off with something incredibly sharp, but there is nothing around the two of them that could've made that precise cut across her long neck, which is making him develop a second emotion of pure confusion. "What just happened? Why am I here? How did my daughter die?", similar and more thoughts kept pouring into his head and filling it up like tap water that won't stop dripping. He tries to keep his usual composure, but how can one when they are looking at a corpse, let alone one's family, flesh and blood? Yasu breaks down slowly but surely, trembling as he sits on his knees in the cold room. He starts crying silent rivers that eventually begins surrounding him on the floor. He crawls to Reina to stretch out his shaking hand and close her eyes that were full of life once upon a lifetime. After some grieving but countless tears, he whispers a final 'I love you' to his deceased daughter before taking up his phone to call the police. However, what Yasu didn't notice is that a coworker had just arrived at the office, witnessing Reina's entire death, including the perpetrator.

"M-murderer!", the coworker shrieks out in fear while pointing harshly at Yasu before running away to warn the others in the building. He does not understand though. Why is Yasu called a murderer? He is still sitting on his knees in a praying position. He was much smarter than this and knew that he had been framed in some way, but that won't stop the sirens he hears outside the building, getting closer and closer. Time doesn't exist anymore for Yasu. All that is left is to pray that justice will be served, for both Reina and him. But considering how the world is looking nowadays, with people getting killed left and right by rumored monsters, the court will most likely believe the media before his own words. If only Yasu knew the fact that he did indeed brutally kill his oldest daughter, Reina Nakashima. Is that the whole and sole truth though?

The police arrive within minutes after getting several emergency messages about a father who turned up only to kill his daughter and a diligent worker at Naka Accounting. The family business was quickly going down in ruins, but that's the least of Yasu's problems. He cannot think or move anymore. All he does while waiting for his dreadful fate behind bars is behaving like a complete apathic man. No tears or feelings are running through his veins, after he realized that there is no God, no matter how much he prays for anything or anyone.

"God doesn't exist," Yasu murmurs to himself in an emotionless tone over and over, making it easy for the police to arrest him on the spot. Frankly, he seemed like a sociopath, and he had every right to act so. He had lost his past already, and now his present and future. What more is there to lose?

As they drive him outside and towards the cars with the sounding sirens, he remains a blank man with a blank mind, even as reporters and journalists begin to surround him to take photos and ask questions. Yasu gets pushed into the passenger seat of one of the vehicles, and as they drive off towards the station, he notices something that makes his eyes go wide. Time starts to go in slow motion, to the point where it completely stops. Yasu looks around with a puzzled look on his face, until he spots something. Outside the window, on the streets, there is a man hidden around the people, blending in with them. He looks young yet old at the same time, if that makes sense, and he is making straight eye contact with the man in the police car. From nowhere, he starts to slowly walk towards the passenger seat. Yasu feels fear bubbling up inside of him the closer the man gets. Luckily for him, the car's doors and windows are locked shut, so the mysterious man cannot get inside anyway. When the man comes close enough for his breath to be seen on the window, his lips form an unnaturally wide smile, stretching from ear to ear. It sends a creepy shiver down Yasu's spine, but from nowhere, the man vanishes, and time starts moving again at normal speed. A fumbled Yasu looks around for the man, but he is gone from sight. Even his breath on the window is gone, like he never existed in the first place. The police officers in the car observes their passenger's eyes, that seems ready to explode, and questions him if something is wrong. Yasu does not want to raise any further suspicions than he already has laid on his shoulders, so he collects himself by wiping some sweat from the brow, letting that gesture be a response to the driver. They shrug it off and continue the journey to the nearest police station. He may be looked down upon as the main suspect of a murder, but a trial is needed nevertheless, after all. The police's radio goes off with a static voice saying, "The trial is ready. I repeat, trial is ready". The words immediately grab Yasu's attention. Trial? Already? The driver responds with a quick and firm "Got it", proceeding with the vehicle in a different direction.

Izumi is doing the usual housework around the nice-looking apartment. Sora is happily playing with his toddler toys while Ayame and Ayaka are in their room, packing clothes and water bottles in smaller bags for the karate lesson that is about to begin in a small building near their place and school, making it easy and practical to travel in between. The mother is humming a song to herself while watering the plants, and that is when their home phone rings. Izumi hurries over to the phone, picks it up and waits for an answer from the other side after answering with a cheerful "Nakashima Residence."

"Good day, ma'am. This is an urgent matter, so I shall cut to the chase. My name is Hibiki Hayakawa and I'm your husband's lawyer. I got informed that he is the law enforcement's main suspect of your daughter that passed away today. They arrested him on the spot, and he has not said a word since, but there is still time to fix this". Izumi didn't comprehend anything the man had just said. It must be wrong number, surely.

"Excuse me, but I think you have gotten the wrong phone number. This is Izumi Nakashima speaking, and though I do have a husband, I don't have a daughter who has passed away," she responds in a collective manner. Hayakawa does a quick sound of sigh before continuing.

"I see... You have not heard about it... It is my deepest apologies that I have to be the one to tell you all of this, Nakashima, and it can most absolutely come as a shock, but Yasu was arrested by the police just now at Naka Accounting for possible aggravated murder of your oldest daughter, Reina Nakashima."

That is indeed a shock for Izumi. A giant one. But it also sends a ton of puzzled questions into her brain. Her dear Yasu would not harm a soul, yet he is accused of killing their Reina. Nothing makes sense… but, after becoming a Behemoth, she has learned lots, including enormous self-control. She keeps her tears away and focuses on, as Hayakawa said, fixing this.

"I must say, I'm kind of in denial, as this doesn't make sense at all… But if Yasu is in trouble for some reason, of course I'll help him!"

"I strongly admire your control over this, Mrs. We must stay as rationally calm as we can to help Yasu out of this. There are solutions to this, so please, do not panic too much too soon. We mustn't think of him as a lost cause."

"Yes… So please, tell me what I can do". Izumi is determined to get him out of the horrible situation he's landed in. Somehow.

"Come down to the police station so we can form a plan. His trial is also about to begin, as he is suspected to be one of the monsters responsible for the Tokyo killings."

That's when Izumi cannot hold back her tears any longer, and almost bursts a shriek out in fear of what they'll do to Yasu if they believe he is a Behemoth! Hayakawa tries to comfort the distraught wife over the phone, and it surprisingly works. She does her best to avoid breaking down and says she'll be at the police station as soon as she can, and the hangs up to cry in silence before collecting herself once more and walk over to the twins' room.

"Ayame, Ayaka! I need to head outside for the day, so cancel your karate lesson and stay home to watch over your little brother, okay?", she hurriedly screams in a lower tone, but loud enough so they can hear every serious word.

"Okaaay!", Ayaka says, cheery and a little oblivious as always. Ayame knows something's going on though. She hears the pain in their mother's voice but does not say anything more that might worsen the situation.

And out to the parking lot Izumi goes. She checks that no one is around and uses her Behemoth speed to hurry up the process of getting there in time. She knows what happens to both discovered Behemoths and humans who believe someone among them is one: a hurried yet legal execution by beheading. She is fully confident and aware that Yasu isn't one of them, but that doesn't matter: If the people believe it, so will the judge. That's unfortunately what this world has come to, overdriven by mad fear of the monsters that are devouring the population. Izumi gets into their dark brown family car and drives off, using her X-Ray vision as help on the road. Everything is "normal", until Izumi sees a shadow in the distance. The shadow reeks of evil and death, making Izumi very suspicious. The closer she gets to it though, the faster it fades away. What could it be? She shakes away the thought of potentially following it; she needs to prioritize getting to her goal! But she cannot truly stop thinking about that person-like shadow in the back of her mind.

"I'm coming, my love…", Izumi whispers over and over to herself. Finally, she's arriving at the police station, but she doesn't see Yasu or anyone who might be Hayakawa. She decides to go inside despite that, telling the receptionist quickly but still in detail about a certain Yasu Nakashima or Hibiki Hayakawa. The woman sitting at the desk informs Izumi that they already are at court, preparing to begin a trial. She takes one big breath and runs out of the entranceway, back into the car and rushing to the Court Hall.

Yasu just arrived, without any knowledge of going straight to trial instead of at least being locked up at the police station to sort things out. The officers put a blanket over his head to avoid photos being taken of his face by journalists and such. They were so desperate to find out if this human really is a monster in disguise. Once they are all inside, the formalities pop up, including Hayakawa politely introducing himself to Yasu as his defendant. Maybe it's just his imagination, but it seems like it's him against the whole room. Except for his lawyer of course. It's all happening so fast, and Yasu is beginning to feel faint from all the pressure. He despises the monsters that he is getting accused of being and has always judged them based on the medias, but now that he is being treated like one himself, he is starting to wonder. Is this retribution, for judging before seeing? He's starting to question everything and everyone from newer perspectives.

"Yasu!", he hears a familiar voice shout out, drenched from the rain that finally is deciding to pour down. It's Izumi.

"Izumi…? What are you- ", he says confusingly but is interrupted by her jumping onto him, giving him the biggest squeeze. She didn't bother paying any attention to her surroundings. She was holding her husband tight with tears in her eyes. She knows what is about to happen to the man she's hugging… and so she decides to give his lips a quick peck, with a taste of sorrowful and bitter salt from the tears that are falling down her eyes, cheeks, nose and lips, as if to connect their souls. Now was the last time to do and say something, anything at all, so she takes this opportunity to reassure Yasu one thing. She whispers her farewells in his ear… and reveals something.

"I'm sorry it's you and not me who got caught. I know what you are, but I also know what I am. You are not one of us, my love. Goodbye," leaving her man in a shock that he is trying to hide and heading for the entranceway. One swift look at the man she came to love but also lie to until his death, and she was walking out the doors. Izumi could not bear to do anything, not even plead. The only thing she could do was to escape the scene and just get away from it all by sitting in the car, alone with her disturbing thoughts. It may seem cold in others' eyes, but Izumi wants to believe that she and Yasu will be okay until the very end if he is aware of the truth of her nature. But it is exactly the truth of her nature that is making everything worse. She slowly begins to see and hear things outside of the car with the help of her X-ray power. Things that weren't there: Just the monster inside her playing mind games with her heart. She just said her farewells to her husband without doing anything to prevent his trial. At the same time, she's thinking in survival mode. It was either Yasu or both Yasu and Izumi, right? If she revealed her true self in order to save him, not only would they have to become fugitives for eternity, but their children would never be able to live normal lives as normal human beings.

Time passes, and Yasu Nakashima's last day here is nearing its end. Izumi is still sitting in their family car at the now empty parking lot. She might not be able to attend the trial, but she has her abnormal X-ray eyes on her side to help her see inside the building and even hear everyone, including Yasu. He is not saying anything though. In fact, he has been quiet as a mouse during the whole thing. His own eyes are looking sleepy, and his mouth hangs slightly open. He doesn't even look conscious. He seems to have reentered that manic state of emptiness, the same state he was in when he saw Reina's head in front of him at the family office department. Yasu knows very well that he is going to face the same fate anytime now, with countless regrets being the last thing being processed in his dying brain. The judge speaks up after quickly going through the new and recent laws that has been put into the rules: "In normal circumstances, Yasu Nakashima would be taken to jail for life, but since he is a suspected Behemoth, with proof outweighing the options, the calls for immediate execution. Therefore, the monster standing before us, shall be executed by beheading. Right here at this moment."

The audience in the hall cheer as Yasu slowly and quietly lets his head fall into death's hands. One quick blow from the executioner and it is over. Time had been slowly but surely stopping for Izumi, and now, for Yasu too. It's like Yasu's decapitated head is rolling on the floor in slow motion while his lifeless body is collapsing onto the floor as a corpse and not a living being anymore. A final tear leaves Yasu's left eye before he goes to another place. A place called Afterlife.

His last words in this world echoes in the big room. "God doesn't exist." Izumi has never felt such complicated pain before. She's feeling the dark, the light, the peace and the chaos, all at the same time. Immediately regretting her decision of letting Yasu go to the next life all alone, she gets a grip with both of her hands on the steering wheel and simply lets her head bang right onto the horn, making the car honk for as long as her body is hanging over the wheel. What emotions are one supposed to feel at a time like this? Not even Izumi knows, despite having been to Hell and back.

"I'm still in denial… Even after seeing you die," she mutters to herself as if speaking with Yasu's spirit while tears run down her red cheeks, like in motion with the pouring rain hitting the windows. Mutters begins escaping the mouth that has a taste of salt from the painful lake in her eyes.

"Did you have to go the way you did? Without saying goodbye to me, or Ayame, or Ayaka, or Sora, or…!", she stops after wanting to say Reina's name. It feels like a taboo word to say out loud now, wrongly enough. What is worse is how she's making it sound: She pretty much made a deal with the devil, leaving him there to handle the situation as he pleases. Izumi honestly can't stop repeating those "what if?" thoughts in her cluttered mind. What if she tried to save him? What if it was worth a try? What if it could change them for the better? What if, what if, what if… But then, a single piece of lightning strikes from the sky, as if an angel had fallen. Izumi lifts her head up instinctively to the crackling sound and looks up to the Heavens. "My dear Reina… My dear Yasu… Are you in pain right now? Are you sad or angry at me? I wouldn't be surprised, after abandoning you two like that… I don't even feel like I deserve to cry for myself," Izumi speaks up in a pained yet soft tone that seems to make the lightning strike once again. She doesn't pay much attention to it at first, but maybe, just maybe, one of them is responding from a faraway place?

"You are my everything, so cry, Izumi. Cry and let your heart speak," a voice as smooth as silk is being heard speaking those words right into Izumi's left ear. She doesn't recognize the voice at all, yet somehow, it feels familiar.

"Yasu…? Is that you?", she manages to say to herself while looking around puzzled but confident, as she is positive that Yasu just spoke to her. From where or how, she can't know. All she wants is a reply, but she isn't getting one, which makes her soul cry endlessly.

And so, after what felt like an eternity of misery, Izumi decides to drive back home. She wipes a final tear away before stepping on the gas.

Ayaka is cheerfully playing with little Sora in the living room, watching television together, while Ayame has herself stuck in their bedroom, at her occupied yet organized desk, her head swimming with thoughts. "What is going on out there?" is the main question that is racing back and forth, with all sorts of possibilities and theories in the mind of the black-haired girl. Of course, unlike her oblivious but optimistic sister, Ayame is much more of a realist and knows when something is going on. She is that 'gifted child' who succeeds with everything in life and has a body and mind full of extreme potential. Grades in school are on top, housework and chores get done quickly, popularity rises like a phoenix out of the ashes… that type of thing. But she has no time to think about all that, as bizarre happenings are clearly occurring in the outside world. It hurts her heart to see this land in this state, since Ayame's life goal is to make this a better place, for both her family and everyone else. Well, the ones that deserve it, at the very least. Some people are simply too good for their own good, but vice versa exists just as much. This is what she wishes to have the righteous power to change one day. It's a far-fetched dream, but you never know, right?

From nowhere, she is disturbed in the middle of her lingering thoughts by lightning striking from far away, but close enough to be able to see it with the naked eye. She hears from the other side of the wall that Sora starts to cry of fear and how Ayaka is nervously trying to come up with toys and such to calm him down. Then, just mere minutes later, another bolt comes down. This one is different though: Somehow, it gives a feeling of warmth and comfort. Even Sora seems to notice this weird sensation, as his crying and complaining stops, little by little. His big eyes show slight hope.

"Aww, Sora, you're such a good boy!", Ayame hear Ayaka exclaim happily while holding the little one in the air and hugging him. When they continue playing with toys, Ayame goes back into her head, but now letting her beautiful, clear blue orbs sit on the window, watching the cloudy rain, confused as to why the lightning bolt felt comforting but also… bittersweet?

A knock on the door and Izumi walks into the apartment, completely drenched from the rain. Both Ayame and Ayaka come to greet their mother while Sora is happily occupied with the television.

"Mother! What happened to you? Did you forget the umbrella? How is it going for big sis and father?", Ayaka starts asking a million questions at the same time out of worry. Ayame knows already enough from their mother's pained face. She doesn't want nor can talk. True enough, not one word escapes her mouth. She hides her tears behind the raindrops on her face.

"I'll run a warm bath for you, mother. Calm down, take your time and come out when you're ready," Ayame says as softly as she can before going into the bathroom. Ayaka is a bit dizzy in the head from the confusion. It seems like her twin sister knows everything about the situation, while little Ayaka stands there and doesn't really know what to say. She's the social type, but what are you supposed to say and do when you don't know anything, with your mother in such a poor condition, on top of that?

"Ayaka… Can you brew me some tea while I wait for the bath…?", Izumi says quietly, but she doesn't lift her head up. She is standing there in the cramped hallway like a zombie, with not much to tell. Ayaka hesitantly nods and heads quickly for the kitchen.

"What kind of tea would you like, mother?"

"… I don't care," Izumi replies right away. She clearly doesn't want to be bothered either. Ayaka regrets asking but continues nevertheless with making some calming chamomile tea. She figures that would be the best option right now. As Ayaka finally decided on which type of tea to brew, Ayame exits the bathroom.

"Relax for as much as you need, mother. Here," Ayame says in a collected tone to the still traumatized Izumi while opening the door for her, where an inviting bubble bath is waiting to cool down her nerves. As soon as the bathroom door closes and locks, Ayaka turns to Ayame, and they start having a whispering conversation.

"Hey… What do you think happened with mother? I've never seen her like this."

"Who knows?"

"Can't you try to talk to her when she gets out, Ayame? You might try to figure something out."

"I don't know, Ayaka. When people want to be left alone, it is best to listen to their choice of isolation."

"But… "

"Just be quiet, Ayaka," Ayame says in an irritated tone. What has suddenly gotten her so frustrated? Was it Ayaka's own curiosity? Or does she know something her own twin sister doesn't know?

Izumi's actions are all pretty apathic. She is removing her overly wet clothes painfully slowly, as if trying to damage the skin with the fabric even further. When they're finally off, she looks at herself in the mirror above the faucet. Izumi is in shock. This can't be right.

"I'm imagining things," she says as quietly as possible to herself, almost too quiet. The thing is, she didn't see herself. In fact, there was no one to look at in the mirror, as it has been painted on to look like a fake mirror. She could not see her own reflection… and she didn't know why. Well, maybe she knew that she literally lost herself along with losing her husband and oldest daughter. Still, she gets creeped out from not seeing herself. It's like she's desperate to find her face again without having to touch it. She hastily goes to the bath water. No reflection there either. How about her body? She hesitantly hugs herself, but the arms go through.

"Am I going mad…? Am I going insane…? Am I going crazy…?", Izumi goes on and on while trying to lay down on the bathroom floor. One moment later, she finds herself going through the floor. The ground. Falling deeper and deeper into the abyss.

That's when she wakes up in a familiar futon. Her own futon. She lets out a sigh of sadness, confusion and relief. "What is reality anymore…"

"Finally awake?", a beautiful voice is heard from the corner of the room. But it is from… the corner of the ceiling? Izumi is dizzy, both in mind and soul, so maybe it is pure hallucination. She wouldn't be surprised if that was the case. Izumi does her best to make her tired body obey her and turn her head towards the voice. It sounds sweet and innocent, but

Izumi doesn't buy it. Something is weird and wrong. She makes sure no one is there and activates her X-Ray vision, just to be certain. Her dark purple eyes light up the room. She looks towards the ceiling, and there is indeed someone there. Izumi freaks out inside: She just revealed herself to be a Behemoth to this stranger!

"Do not fear: We're on the same side. Well, sort of. I have information to share, but I guess it'll have to wait. I'll see you some other day and time, mother."

The voice is now coming from behind her. Izumi hastily turns around and sees... who is this Behemoth?

"I'll put you back to sleep now."

Izumi tries to speak but just as she is about to ask for an identity, she disappears into the world of dreams once again.

An exhausted Izumi is woken up by two worried daughters surrounding her. Ayaka is on the verge of crying and Ayame goes to find something and quickly comes back with a tiny bucket filled with water and a towel hanging from it. Ayame dips the towel carefully in the lukewarm water and puts it on their mother's forehead. As soon as Ayaka sees that she is awake, or at least half-awake, she tightly hugs Izumi. She groans in pain a bit.

"It... hurts, Ayaka..."

"Just leave her to rest, Ayaka. I know you're happy she survived that fall in the bathroom, but we need to take care of her wounds and well-being first. She's most likely confused anyways from hitting her head," Ayame slightly scolds her sister. Ayaka apologizes and backs off while wiping away her newfound tears.

"What happened to me...?", a confused Izumi asks her daughters.

"After you went into the bathroom, I heard you slip and fall on the tile floor. Ayaka was playing with Sora, so she didn't hear it, but I heard it loud and clear, so I took a small knife to unpick the lock, put a towel around you and dragged your body in here. Now that you know, just rest," Ayame explains directly and firmly. Ayaka seems like she wants to talk again, so she opens her mouth to speak.

"You were squirming around in your sleep. Did you have a nightmare, mother?", this clicks a memory from the dream where an unknown Behemoth called her exactly that. She sits up drastically and mutters to herself.

"Mother?!"

"What...? Are you okay, mother?", says the now confused Ayaka. She tries to put a gentle hand on the shaken up's fragile shoulder.

"Don't touch me! Please... just don't," Izumi says, first with an aggressive tone, but then realizes she's talking to her own daughter and calms down a bit. Ayame stands up and approaches Ayaka with irritated words once more.

"Ayaka, I told you, she's confused and needs to rest! Let her recover! Ugh..."

Izumi's thoughts go wild while the sisters are bickering. She looks fuzzily at them, one by one, as if analyzing them. Why did she connect a Behemoth with her children? Well, she only has one answer to that. Worst case scenario, one of them is a Behemoth. That can't be it, but it's possible, considering she herself is one. But they're twins: Wouldn't both be Behemoths then? Maybe they are not aware of it, in that case? No, when it's a female Behemoth and a human having twins, even then is it always a 50% chance that one child can come out a pure human and the other a pure monster. She's trying to figure out more fragments from the dream, and after remembering it all, she now needs to choose who to trust. She never thought she would have to distrust her own child, but...

... Is the Behemoth Ayaka or Ayame?

I'll have to dissect every move and word from them from now on. It could get me clues, Izumi thinks.

It's been some time since Izumi woke up. She explained everything that she knew to her daughters, except the obvious fact that she is of Behemoth blood. Izumi had no choice but to tell it all eventually, but with white lies here and there. Partly to hide her true self, partly to hide the fact that she knows one of her children are hiding their identity as well. She must figure out who, why and how. Who is in the darkness, why they're in the darkness and how they came into the darkness: All of these things needs answers, so Izumi has spent the last days and weeks processing the family deaths with the twins. Ayame was not surprised at all, since the mysterious murders has been going on for a longer time, so she knew it could happen to the dearest people in her life too. The fact that Ayame was mentally prepared for the horrible news is both normal and strange. Ayaka though... she was erratic in sadness, fear, anger, and whatever more negative emotions you could possibly feel after hearing family members died, especially Reina who believed in Ayaka more than anyone. Ayaka is never afraid to show her emotions and share her thoughts, and this was no exception. But she calmed down unusually quickly, which was weird too.

Izumi doesn't know how to take the girls' reactions. It's like they've switched traits, in some ways. Ayaka and Ayame are even spending less time with each other, which is highly unusual for twins to begin with. Days go by with Izumi analyzing everything they say and do without giving herself away in the process. At this point, both could be Behemoths, or both could be humans. Maybe she should just confront them, like a mother is meant to do? 'It's worth a try,' she thinks to herself hesitantly but determined to find out more about the two she thought she knew the most about.

"Can I come in?", Izumi asks while facing their shared bedroom and knocking lightly on the door. The door goes ajar as Ayaka opens it and shows a genuine and inviting smile. In there are Ayame and Sora, and giggles cover up the whole room. Ayaka, Ayame and the little one is clearly having fun with using Ayame's many drawing and painting materials to let Sora's explosive creativity go off. Izumi join their small laughers instinctively.

"So, this is where my Sora has been hiding! With his sisters, huh?", she exclaims happily to Sora while lifting him up and giving him a hug. Izumi now remembers why she got in there to begin with, after seeing Sora's face. She never really thought about it, but he really resembles Yasu. She cautiously puts Sora down, clears her throat and gets the girls' attention that way.

"How are you two holding up? I mean, with everything that has happened. You haven't been going to school or your karate lessons because of… the rumors of your father. I want to make sure you all are safe," a serious mother says while looking her daughters in their clear blue eyes. The twins look at each other in the corner of the eye before Ayame decide to speak.

"We are as okay as can be, considering the circumstances. I think I can talk for both myself and Ayaka when I say that you don't have to worry about us. We will make it."

"I see. What about you, Ayaka? Do you agree?"

"Mhm! Just take care of yourself, mother," Ayaka adds into the conversation.

"Okay. How about… well, how do I put this…" Izumi must think twice before she says anything further, so she doesn't come off as suspicious. "You two will turn 18 years old this year. November 16th may be far away, as we are just getting introduced to summer, but still… How do you think about yourselves now? What do you want to do in the future, for example?" Izumi discreetly tries to get clues out of the girls in front of her. They're quite confused though, then they look at each other and Ayaka smug while Ayame looks away with a slight blush.

"Mother… are you trying to ask us about our love lives? How rude!", Ayaka teasingly tells Izumi while looking all smug. Okay, they've got the wrong idea and didn't give useful answers. Ayaka answered as the usual Ayaka would, but Ayame never thinks about romance. Izumi gets curious to whether Ayame is hiding something or has simply found a good guy who understands her. She is popular in school, after all.

Izumi decides to play along with Ayaka's silly idea. I mean, hey, Izumi used to be lovestruck in their age too: she'll understand something if they open their box that are in their hearts.

"Yes, that's right! I'd like to know if any of you has found someone to spend the rest of their lives with. Passing everything onto the next generation is important, you know! Family, friends, education, and so on. Right?"

"I have no interest whatsoever in romance, nor do I believe in true love. I was surprised by the question, that is all," Ayame strictly tells both

Ayaka and Izumi, leaving them speechless that a wonderful young woman like Ayame does not want anything to do with the subject.

"Even if you found your Prince Charming?", Ayaka shyly says, her smug smile slowly disappearing at the sudden offense in her sister's voice. This time, she answers in a more downhearted tone.

"There is no Prince Charming... Not for me..."

"But—"

"Let me believe in my own ideology!", Ayame aggressively almost screams out. She clearly is mad at the topic, maybe even offended. That's when Izumi notices something that could be gravely important. It is very faint, but she swore that she just saw Ayame's eyes turn... dark purple?

"Ayame...? Dear...?", Izumi softly tries to calm her down, whether what she saw was real or not. But that's when Ayame storms out of the room, leaving behind a confused toddler, twin and mother. Izumi decides that she cannot stop here though. She needs to find out if what she witnessed was the truth! And thus, she goes after Ayame, looking desperately in every room until she enters the master bedroom, Izumi's own room, and the air feels different. She gets a hunch that it's the same, or at least similar, to the special dream she had, so she looks into the standing mirror in the corner of the room. There is no reflection to look at, again. She looks at the windows, but there is nothing to see from outside. From nowhere, the room turns pitch black. Izumi activates her X-Ray to try to find herself in the dark, but it has no effect.

"That won't work. In here, only my eyes can guide the world." Izumi recognizes the voice. It's the same voice from before, so she is in that strange dream! But how did she get there? It's not like she slipped and fell again.

"Where are you?!", Izumi says with a threatening voice.

"Here, mother. I'm here," the voice replies calmly.

As the voice is beginning to sound more and more familiar, she turns around slowly, and sees two big, dark purple orbs right behind her. It feels like the glare is suffocating Izumi: This is a Behemoth, but the strongest one she has ever encountered. How does a Behemoth get so overpowerful in the first place? It is completely overbearing. Fear takes over Izumi and she turns away from the only light source in there, but just as she turns around, she hears a swift in the air and the purple eyes are in front of her now. Too fast for Izumi! She feels like she might die if she stays in here, so she quickly asks one question to make it clear, once and for all.

"Who are you?"

"Me? I'm nobody. Well, I do have a rather famous name related to my real name. You, who are a Behemoth too, must know of Crimson Purple."

"Crimson Purple? As in the Crimson Purple princess?"

"Correct. That is I."

"I thought you only were a fairytale in storybooks for Behemoths to read to their children, just like humans read the story of princess Kaguya to their families. I suppose nothing surprises me anymore."

"Am I frightening to you, mother?"

"No."

"Liar."

"Wait, why are you calling me 'mother'? It should be the opposite, if anything."

"I'll turn a light on, if you decide to stay in this world temporarily to listen to my life. Just for you, mother." Izumi takes a minute to think if this is right: Her presence is scary enough as it is. Can she trust the princess? Eventually, Izumi nods and sits down on the floor. The princess closes her eyes to sit in front of Izumi, while the room is getting clearer and clearer, at least the aura around the Crimson Purple princess. It's a pure, ghost white. She makes a candlelight appear in her hand, lights it by blowing at it and puts it in front of her so Izumi can look at who the voice belongs to. It's a petite young lady, dressed in a unique traditional dress, a mixture of purple, black and white. Her long, black hair goes down to the floor. It also has a crimson-colored rose in it, along with a matching necklace. She's incredibly beautiful and beyond anything Izumi has ever seen, heard or read about.

"Hello, mother," Ayame says while opening her eyes, revealing the plausible dark purple orbs.

CHAPTER III

"So, it really was you, Ayame. I have so many questions. I'm just in shock that you are the actual Crimson Purple princess. I don't know much about the story, but she is a holy being who will save the world, right?" Izumi comments with wide open eyes, staring back at the young woman who is standing before her. It looks like an extremely refined Ayame, a side she's never seen before from her. But she is indeed beyond beautiful, inside and out, so the whole 'I am Crimson Purple' must be true. Izumi has taught herself lots of self-control and is trying her best to compose herself.

"I'll tell you how it all began. I'll only show you once, so pay attention."

"Show me?" And then, in a second, Izumi is reviewing flashbacks and visions from other times she doesn't recognize. They go on like an old film, showing one picture after the other while Ayame tells her story.

"The humane story about princess Kaguya is true, but what all of humanity has left out and forgotten is the fact that the princess had a twin. A twin sister with no name, as she was viewed as a monster right at birth, so she was simply called the Crimson Purple princess. A monster princess with one dark purple eye and one crimson red. She became feared without even trying by all except her sister, Kaguya. Everyone knew Kaguya would be the successor out of the two of them, including Crimson Purple, but Kaguya created a rebellion and did not take the throne, for the sake of her sister, whom had been shunned out by everybody, despite being better than her twin in all ways, ironically enough. She was beyond anything you could ever imagine. Just from appearance, many young men fell for her, but were too scared of her overly strong power and enticing beauty."

"Question, Ayame. What did Crimson Purple look like?"

"Exactly like my appearance. Look at her and look at me: Identical, is it not?", Ayame says while holding out her hand, which shows a slightly hovering picture of the Crimson Purple princess. Just like Ayame said, they are like identical twins. Long black hair, pale-white skin, and so on... there's only one thing that does not match, but Izumi decides to hold that thought. She thinks she knows where this story is headed, based on what she knows about Behemoth's ancient history. Ayame continues. "When princess Kaguya decided to flee to Earth, she asked if princess Crimson Purple wanted to come with her. Start a new life, hiding their identities together. She agreed, and both princesses came down to Earth like two shooting stars. Humanity already existed down there, so naturally, some saw the princesses. They did not know the Japanese language at first though, making it difficult to understand one another. The humans invited them to see their land's emperor, and surely enough, Kaguya fell in love with the human emperor and bore his children. She became an empress anyway. Crimson Purple felt like she was unwanted here too, until one night when she met a traveler in the darkness. "Finally, I found you, holy princess Crimson Purple.", he said in their own language while going down on his knees, begging her to marry him. He was quite handsome for a human, but how did he know about her? Simple: Word spread across the lands like wildfire that a heavenly woman with a purple eye and a crimson eye had come down from another world. She was so moved that a human would fall for her without being afraid and decided to stay by his side. Kaguya did not like this though: After giving birth to human twins, she became jealous of Crimson Purple on an extreme level. Her arrogance took over and she eventually tried to destroy the Earth, including her own sister. The traveler, who turned out to be the emperor's brother, decided to go hand in hand with Crimson Purple to the emperor and tell him everything, including how Kaguya has been gone from the land to plot a world destruction. The emperor became enraged of his wife's decision and told everyone in the lands to look for her to kill Kaguya. Princess Crimson Purple wanted to take care of this alone though, and so she ventured and found Kaguya at the spot where they arrived when coming here to Earth. An intense battle occurred, which Crimson Purple won, but instead of killing her own twin sister, she sealed her away high up in the sky, which is today known as the moon. After that, Crimson Purple became known as the Goddess of the Sun. She lived happily here until death."

Izumi is stunned by the story. It sounds like a fairytale that is too good to be true. But what she doesn't understand is why Ayame is telling her any of this.

"Another question, Ayame. How is this related to you? If this story really is true, it happened millennials ago. Why is it something you should know?" Ayame's answer is a hand gesture: She put the palm of her head on her eye, waited a few seconds, and when she removed her hand, the eye had changed color from dark purple to crimson red.

"Because I have the Crimson Purple princess' blood in me. I am her descendant and prophecy."

"Prophecy...? What do you mean?", Izumi asks quizzingly. She herself is not of any royal or abnormal blood, so how could this be?

"While the original Crimson Purple, the Goddess of the Sun, was alive, she tried but could never get pregnant. Thus, she chose that there would be a successor in the far future. A future she couldn't even dream of. The princess was full of hope that her successor would continue protecting the world, saving it when it's in need for saving. Mother... That time is now. I am the successor of the gifted goddess. I am now Crimson Purple," Ayame says excitedly while gently taking Izumi's hands and holding them in her own cold hands. Izumi has no words. All her questions disappear from her mind. This cannot be happening, can it? That her daughter is the savior of this world?

"I... don't know what to say, Ayame. I really don't."

"You don't have to, either. Just believe in me and help me hide my identity from everyone, including Ayaka. I highly doubt it, but history can always repeat itself. Trust me: I will save Japan from its curse."

"... Okay," Izumi gives a flat answer. She doesn't know if this is real or fake, but it seems too real to be fake, so she decides to have faith in her Behemoth daughter who, supposedly, will save the world.

"My time is running out. He might find out about this if we stay here for too long, so let's go back to reality. I'll make sure you remember everything. Just pretend that everything is as it normally is. Please."

"Who is 'he'?"

Before she knows it, Izumi is outside the fabricated dimension Ayame had created and back to the real world. Ayame is still in her traditional clothing, with her eyes activated, but quickly enough changes within a snap of the fingers to change her whole appearance. Back to black but shorter hair, her blue eyes and her type of normal clothing. She puts a finger to her lips, as if saying 'this is our secret'. Izumi is hesitating though. Surely Ayaka would understand, so why not tell? It's like Ayame told only the ancient history and not much about herself. What powers does she have in her arsenal? If she's really the prophecy, she should be overpowered, but there is no way Izumi can know more in detail the story behind the story. Either way, she sure won't go around and calling her own daughter a goddess or a princess, even though Izumi is beginning to believe it and take it seriously. Human or not, no one would or should have to lie about their true selves. Izumi has always been a realistic optimist, especially with things and people she cares about. She has no real reason to distrust Ayame, nor has Ayame a basis of lying. Izumi and Yasu raised their children to strictly live truthfully and righteous lives, telling them to always follow both the mind and heart at the same time to find a healthy balance. That's why Yasu, as a father, did not expect daughter Ayaka to become the typical carefree girl. In secret, he was constantly proud of her and watching over her, nevertheless. Now he's watching over his children too of course; just in a different way and place. 'Yasu, dear… why did you have to leave now…?', Izumi thinks while letting out a sad sigh before Ayaka suddenly hurries into the room.

"Ayame! You didn't have to be so dramatic!"

"Don't worry, Ayaka. We just had a little chat and Ayame has calmed down," Izumi says nervously, hoping Ayaka doesn't catch them in the half-lie. She might be carefree but she's not dumb. Luckily enough, she shrugs it off.

"Okay. I'm just glad you're fine now, Ayame. Don't scare me like that."

"Sorry, Ayaka," Ayame politely apologies with a slight bow.

"Well, I'm going to little Sora. He's probably missing you, so tag along!", she says, and turns and goes.

"I'll be right behind you," Ayame confirms with a small smile and wave. As soon as the sister is gone, Izumi puts a hand on Ayame's shoulder, and asks something she just need to know.

"She's not one of us, is she?"

"No, she is not. I would have felt it otherwise right away."

"Wait, does that mean you knew all along about me?", Izumi asks apprehensively.

"I've always known about you," Ayame replies, and now silence is laying itself over the bedroom. After a minute or two, Izumi asks one final thing before Ayame heads off to go play with her siblings.

"Everything is going to get tough now, won't it?"

Ayame activates her crimson and dark purple eyes for a moment, looking intensely into Izumi's eyes.

"It won't be tough. It will be brutal," she says while deactivating her eyes. Off the new Crimson Purple goes. Izumi is standing still in terror. She really, truly believed every single word Ayame said just by looking into her penetrating eyes. She knew exactly what Izumi was asking, and she gave Izumi the deadly answer.

She decided to get on with the day as if nothing has happened. Processing complicated matters takes time, and this is no exception. As she is cooking and preparing for a nice dinner, stuffed cabbage rolls with rice and miso soup, she can hear the three siblings in the other room and how much fun they seem to have. This gives Izumi, as a loving mother, a more optimistic and hopeful view for the future. At least for the near future, since she does not know how every tomorrow will look like from now on. One day at a time sounds like a good idea.

The day is gone, and night has taken over Tokyo. It's a clear, moonlit sky tonight. The light is finding itself creeping into the apartment. Eventually, the silhouette of a rather suspicious man with a long black coat is slowly showing itself outside the twins' bedroom. Ayame, who was sleeping peacefully a few seconds ago, is now awake. She looks completely awake and aware, as if she had never gone to sleep in the first place. She gets up and heads to the window. She looks at the shady man and whispers to herself a disappointing "really?" before, with the snap of her fingers again, transforming clothes. This time, she is wearing black & white sporty sneakers, along with black shorts and a long-sleeved shirt that is blending itself into the rest of the attire, as it is colored purple at the top but heading towards black at the end of it. She is also wearing fishnet stocking protection at her elbows and kneecaps. Her nails are painted in different shades of sensual red. She gives a raw look as she fulfills her outfit with activated eyes. A frightening dark purple. She nods to the man and his figure fades away. When she feels ready, Ayame opens the window, closes it behind her and disappears into the breezy night. "No one is outside at times like these anymore, but you never know," Ayame says to herself while teleporting small distances so potential humans don't see her running down the apartment complex's outer wall at superhuman speed. "If he called me out now, it must mean there's someone nearby doing it," she continues talking to herself while activating her eyes. As a living prophecy, Ayame's powers outstands any other lesser or greater Behemoth. She can do everything the original princess Crimson Purple could. Of course, she is not an immortal: Even for a monster, immortality is and will always be impossible to acquire. She is simply the strongest creature in Japan (and probably this world) right now.

Ayame is jumping from building to building quickly, almost frantically, while keeping a straight face. The only thing you can see in the moonlight is Ayame's glowing eyes, ready to hit her jackpot. She's clearly searching for something but cannot seem to find it... until Ayame sees an incident in a karaoke bar to be wary about.

"Bingo."

Ayame hurries down to the ground and walks in. The young man, who is apparently the receptionist, gets startled at the sight of such a beautiful young woman.

"W-welcome. Room for one, I assume?", the receptionist says and bows politely, flustered. However, Ayame decides to ignore him and walk towards the smell of alcohol in the room further away. The receptionist sits down at the desk, sighing at his missed opportunity. He fixes his glasses and continues with his lazy job, while Ayame continues with hers. She goes down the right hallway with firm steps. It's as if the hall is shaking with every step she takes. The tension arises, and just as she is ready to storm inside, a quick shriek is heard from the karaoke room. Ayame realizes she is too late. She opens the door and in there is a colorful crime scene. A drunken man in his middle 40s holding a cracked beer bottle with sharp, red edges. In front of him is a small splash of blood, and in the middle of it is a girl around Ayame's age lying down, completely passed out from a clumsy but hard hit in the head. Most likely was it the man's bloodied bottle that caused her bleeding. The older man hit her several times, considering the amount of the splattered red that is blending in with the karaoke room's walls. Ayame is stunned with anger. Just as she is about to act, the receptionist runs into the room after hearing the scream. He doesn't know what to do after seeing the man standing over the bloody young lady, thus turning to run back to the desk to dial 110, Japan's emergency number. Ayame realizes the whole thing will get very complicated if the police arrive now, especially with her here, so she decides to run up to the guy and take a hold of his head, with her whole hand strongly staying on his forehead. She stays like that for a few seconds or so, with the 45-year-old man dumbfounded, both from the strange gesture and from the alcohol in his blood.

"W-what're you doing, lady?", the drunken one loudly asks.

"Removing his most recent memories. I don't want to get caught up in a sticky situation," Ayame flatly responds.

"Removing memories…? Have you had a beer too, lady?" No response this time. After she's done and the manly worker collapses on the floor, Ayame checks the pulse of the woman in danger. Nothing. She's stone cold, gone forever.

"She's dead."

"What…? She didn't want me! So… yeah," the man says while opening another bottle of beer.

"Little do you know… that that is your final drink, old man," Ayame says in a raw and furious tone, before teleporting behind him and sinking her teeth into the drunk man in an instant. He does not have time to react before he dies faster than his much younger victim. The blood tastes disgusting yet sweet at the same time. Most likely the alcohol's cause. "I don't think I have ever had an easier kill. Thanks for the tasty meal, assaulter," Ayame says after sucking every single drop of blood from the now dead man. She lets his body fall to the floor while she prepares to leave for the night. She says a final "I'm sorry I couldn't save you" to the deceased girl, and jumps away from there, back to her family's apartment. She walks up to the complex, towards her bedroom window, goes in and gets back in bed without anyone noticing. Or so she thinks: Izumi has, in truth, been awake the whole time. Not only is she awake, but she is also disturbed after witnessing everything that happened in the karaoke bar with her X-Ray vision. To not raise any suspicions, the mother continues laying down on her bed futon, with both her head and heart quizzing her. Why did her daughter use her powers for evil? She's the holy being who is supposed to save this world, so why is she taking a turn in her actions like this? Ayame has always been a serious but sweet girl. Izumi thought she understood her daughter, but it seems that was not the case, after all. 'I'll confront her in the morning,' is the last thought Izumi has before her eyelids becomes heavy enough to let her fall asleep.

The alarm clock at the small bedside table goes off; 6:30 AM. Now, the twins are going back to karate lessons and school life. They have been allowed by their understanding principal to study from home after what happened to their father, but they must be fully prepared for the final exams now that the end of their education is getting closer and closer, so back to normality it is. Ayaka takes 5 more lazy minutes in the bed before getting up.
"Man, my body is stiff from being home all day! It'll be nice to go back to karate!", Ayaka jumps out of bed excitedly and stretches while saying this loudly, as if trying to wake up Ayame. But she's still in bed.
"Ayame? You awake?" Finally, Ayame groans a bit while turning to look at Ayaka with sleepy eyes.
"My apologies, sister. I'm tired, so I think I'll skip out on practice today." This makes Ayaka frown with a disappointed facial expression.

"Please…?", Ayaka begs with puppy eyes. Then, Izumi comes in after overhearing their short chit-chat.

"Ayame's right. She's still mentally exhausted, so let her relax for the day, Ayaka." Ayaka tries to protest her mother's words, saying that this isn't like Ayame, but Izumi makes believable excuses to get the carefree twin to the karate practices before she's late. She gets a casual outfit on, just a hot pink tank top with white shorts, packs a backpack with her karate attire, a water bottle and other necessities before heading out into the day. Today is warm and sunny, with occasional clouds in the otherwise spotless sky.

When Izumi has made sure Ayaka is out of sight and reach, she decides for the confrontation to take place.

"Why did you let her go without me, mother?", Ayame quizzingly asks.

"Don't play dumb with me, Ayame. I saw everything from this night. Explain yourself," an angered Izumi exclaims. "How could you kill someone?!", she adds, but she's not getting an expected response from her daughter.

"Oh, so you saw it with your X-Ray vision. This must be my lucky day! I've been wanting to show you more about my duties and such, but it seems like there never was a time for us to sit down and talk it through and through!", Ayame is excited, and you can hear it from her voice. In fact, she gets so excited that she accidentally activates her crimson red and dark purple eyes.

"Ayame… Your eyes…", Izumi says with a disturbed tone while pointing at her eyes.

"My bad, my bad! I'm just so happy that you saw everything." She really is ecstatic. It's as if she's role-playing with herself as a crazy killer. Which is half-true, if you look at it from the right angle, but Izumi is doubting those negative thoughts. She is just confused and needs to hear Ayame's version of the truth.

"Why did you do it?"

"Because he deserved to die. Simple." She looks at her mother with gleaming yet lifeless eyes and tells her these things while sitting comfortably on the floor with her head resting on her hand, as if she's bored. "You see, mother… some humans are simply unworthy. Of this life, that is. They are naïve, arrogant and selfish. There are a small portion of good people in this world though. They are who I'm trying to save. I'm salvation. I'm Crimson Purple's legend."

"That doesn't mean you can go off killing innocent humans like that, no matter their ideals and goals in life!", an angered Izumi tells her daughter. She is accepting what she's hearing but that doesn't mean she wants to believe it. Not yet. Thus, she decides to suppress her anger for now and listen to her story, like she told herself that she would do.

"It seems you have gotten the wrong idea, mother. I'm not killing innocent human beings. I would never do such a thing. The lives that I take are people who have traded with the devil. They take life for granted and abuse it by sexually assaulting women of all ages for their own pleasure. When filthy rapists don't get what they want, what do they do? They do what you witnessed this night. They all turn into monsters; monsters worse than you or I will ever be. We haven't done anything, after all. If you look back and think a little, I'm sure you'll stop giving me that disappointed look and understand my point of view," Ayame continues while giving a suspicious smile. Izumi knows right away what she's talking about: She herself got raped by Ichirou Fukui, Yasu's rival who died by Izumi's hands, and that is how she became a mutation of what she is today. She immediately looks down on the floor and makes a pained face, remembering all the gibberish Ichirou told her after almost killing her with the brutal action.

"Are you reminiscing the pain, the blood, the regret?", a soft and sympathetic voice from Ayame is heard. Izumi is still looking down on the ground. Tears are forming in her eyes, and now she is the one who makes her eyes, blue as the sky, transform slowly into a teary purple shade. Ayame stands up, stands in front of the woman in painful waterfalls and puts two comforting hands on her shoulders, pulling her head up, making them have an emotional connection as their activated eyes meets each other in a tear-jerking stare. Ayame does something she hasn't ever done with anyone around: She sobs. Quietly.

"It was rough, wasn't it…? Especially how they always get away with their sins… No one deserves a trauma like this. Not you… and not me." Her crying gets louder and more erratic, while Izumi's tears stop for a second, as she thought she heard her daughter say something very strange.

"Did you just say… that you've been through it too?"

"By the most powerful, frightening man. I was a small child who knew nothing of this world nor myself. All I remember is that it hurt, and still hurts to this day."

"Oh, my dear Ayame…", Izumi sadly exclaims and invites her in for a hug, which Ayame agrees to. They stand there for a minute, crying on each other's shoulders, before Izumi dramatically pulls away and looks her daughter, once again, in the eyes. This time, a murderous feeling has interrupted Izumi's sanity and it's visible in her own orbs. She needs to know who did it, so she can find him and make him pay with blood. She lets her killer nature take over and demands Ayame to tell her who, but the young woman… smiles?

"That's the feeling. That's the kind of look I am required to live with, for I am Crimson Purple's legacy, and I'm not going to let another being become a victim. A sin is a sin. All the filthy rapists deserve Death's ruthless knock on their pitiful doors."

"TELL ME WHO IT IS, AYAME!" Izumi is in a maniac-like state. Her true self starts to stand out by the looks of her tiger-like teeth, the small horns that has rapidly grown out and the voice of a real monster. Ayame is gazing at the furious thing in front of her. This is a Behemoth. Someone who is meant to be hated and feared above all. But, for Ayame, this is a wonder to look at. She cups Izumi's cheeks in her slender hands.

"You look beautiful, mother. I'll tell you, but only if you help me. The group needs all the saviors it can get."

Izumi calms down, slowly but assumingly enough. "Group?"

CHAPTER IV

I close my eyes as instructed, letting my blue orbs fall underneath the eyelids. After deep focus, I drastically open my eyes. I can feel the activation of the crimson red and dark purple. Suddenly, I'm standing in a void, with a golden key in my right hand and a black door in front of me. I walk over to the big, ancient door and unlock it. As I coolly walk in, I'm greeted with polite, deep bows from a small group of people. They are wearing black and white clothing that looks just as old as the door. Everyone in the huge room is also wearing individual masquerade masks, as if this were a costume party. I cannot tell who they are, but they're like me. I can tell from their eyes: Some have dark purple, some have ruby red, and some even have one golden yellow eye on their left and a dusty grey on the right one. I can also see that they're all kinds of different builds, genders and ages, and almost everybody is beyond good-looking. No one seems to have my eye colors though.

"Welcome, holy Crimson Purple princess," they all say as I walk slowly down the room. Observing the place, it looks like a smaller sanctuary, with different rooms occupying the space. One for dining, another for sleeping and so on. Suddenly, a strange shadow appears before me. The shadow becomes slightly more visible when it has reached its final form; a manly figure with red eyes staring right at me, but nothing more can be told just by this.

"Welcome to the sanctuary for Behemoths, new princess. This is a secret place far from humans where everything and everyone are safe to do whatever they like. I often make… events."

"You mean hunting bad people down?"

"Yes, my child, that is an excellent way to put it! Her talent, her beauty! Everybody, admire it!"

In the current room of the sanctuary, the main hall, I look around, confused yet not, after hearing the people start repeating 'Princess Ayame!' in ecstatic tones while still holding their heads down. From nowhere, the shadowy man makes a hand motion towards me, making me wear similar clothing as the others. A huge, elegant dress in white and black with accessories and nail polish in shades of crimson and purple. The shadow makes another hand gesture to make a rose appear in his almost invisible hands, then placing the red flower in my hair. I truly feel like a princess in her right place. Everybody accepts- no, worships me. I have some questions for the man though, as this is all still very new to me. It is my first time here, after all.

"Shadow man?"

"Yes, milady?"

"Why do I have different eye colors now?"

"Ah... You see, our pupils transform color when we activate our abnormal abilities. Blue shall become dark purple, brown shall become ruby red, green shall become golden yellow on the left iris and dusty grey on the right one. Fascinating, is it not?"

"... Hmm," I say quietly while muttering to myself with one hand holding my chin.

"What a sophisticated young princess we have!"

"Me?"

"Yes, you, Ayame Nakashima," the shadow man says in an almost seductive voice while kneeling to kiss my other hand.

"That was the memories of the first time I met the group, and my first memory that I can recall from this life. Everything else is gone. This was just after I had gotten raped," Ayame says while letting go of Izumi's head. Her mother got to see her daughter's memories to try to find out more about Ayame and this group of hers. She has a bit more insight of it now, but what disturbs her is that shadowed man.

"I don't understand... who, or what, is the shadow man?"

"I may be a passing legend, but not even I know who he is. All I'm aware of is that he introduced himself as the leader of the group and the strongest male Behemoth living. Sometimes curiosity take over though, and every time I try to secretly investigate him, my heart starts hurting badly, as if someone is squeezing it hard." Izumi's eyes widen while she's trying to think like a detective looking for clues in her mind.

"The way he talked... the way he described the eye colors..."

"Mother?" Ayame is slightly confused, as Izumi is muttering to herself, perhaps even without realizing. A nerve looks like it's about to pop. She's focusing that much.

"What if... No, that's impossible..."

"Mother."

"Maybe I never finished the job... maybe I didn't look close enough..."

"Mother!", and now Izumi snaps back.

"Oh, I'm sorry, Ayame! I'm just thinking."

"Out loud."

"Sorry, sorry. You know I like to hum and mutter all sorts of things to myself. Don't worry about it." Ayame knows something is up with her mother but decides to ignore it; she notices that Izumi wants to collect her thoughts first before forming a sentence.

"Hey, Ayame... May I meet the leader of the group, the shadow man?" Izumi expects nothing less than an astounding 'yes', but what she gets is a suspicious 'why?'. She needs to sound much better than that if someone like Ayame is going to buy it.

"I need to know more if I'm going to join the group, you know. Although it looked more like a cult in my head." Silence for a minute or two. Ayame has her eyes closed and is whispering without pronouncing the words, as if chanting a spell. Then, she opens to reveal her different-colored orbs.

"I just spoke with the shadow man. He'll let you see everyone, including him and the sanctuary. If you'd like, of course."

"I'd love to!" Izumi is surprised that Ayame is letting her. Well, maybe she knows but is hiding it. Izumi doesn't believe her own child would put her in a trap, but she really needs to be wary of this mysterious man. She can only think of one Behemoth as powerful as Ayame, but he's gone, so that theory is probably out of the question. Who can it be? Only one way to find out.

"The time in the other world goes the same as in reality. Thus, we need to find a plausible place to perform the small ritual. We might be in there for a long time, and Ayaka must not see it," Ayame says, as serious as can be.

"What happens if Ayaka catches us?"

"Not only would we have a lot of explaining to do, but she could get sucked into that void and discover everything. I'm not taking any chances, mother. Are you?"

Izumi shakes her head. She just hopes that, once she visits the sanctuary, she won't have to do something she promised herself not to ever do again: Kill someone.

Months passes by without much happening. The days are hot from the burning August sun, and dull from everything being the same. Ayame said she would tell Izumi when they have a good enough opportunity to go to the void, but nothing has been heard from her. She and Ayaka has been busy studying hard for the final exams before graduation, which they obviously passed. It was to be expected from both and Izumi is incredibly proud of them. Now that Ayame and Ayaka are done with school, unless they want to seek further education, they just sit at home and are relaxing with the summer weather. Sora is growing up too, bit by bit. He's learnt how to talk, walk and have a sense of reality completely, especially thanks to big sis Ayaka. Ayame has been sitting at her desk, practicing her calligraphy and other forms of traditional art, wanting to become something in the creative field. She has still been going on "missions" occasionally though. Izumi figured out that it is the shadow man who contacts her, most often in the night, when there are victims of assaulters out there, so the newspapers always have something to write about. However, the fact that Izumi's daughter is going around and killing human beings, no matter how filthy they are, makes her stomach turn. She must keep up the act though, at least until it is time to strike.

In the middle of August, the twins' school decides to celebrate their now graduated students with a tiny but final school trip to Fukuoka, as a present for the most gifted ones and families. As Ayame and Ayaka gets picked out for the trip, since they were one of the top students, Ayame thinks of this as the perfect opportunity and therefore encourages Ayaka to take Sora to see the outside world. Izumi, knowing that that is Ayame's signal, agrees and prepares everything before they head out with cute shrieks of happiness.
"Okay, they're gone," Izumi confirms with grave importance. Ayame nods, "Let us begin then."

"This is an exhausting ritual for beginners. You, who are a mutation, will have an even harder time. It might seem difficult, but you will get it if you're paying attention. Watch now." Ayame sits down with her legs crossed and places her intertwined hands to rest between her legs. She looks like she's meditating: Every motion is very, very slow. She is even taking her time closing her eyes. Izumi is observing every step and writing it down in her mind. It is honestly mesmerizing to watch Ayame. She breathes in and out one time, and then, quick as ever, opens her now crimson red and dark purple orbs widely. An intense fog is immersing Ayame's body, and when she stands up and lets the fog go away, she looks completely different. She has her traditional clothing on: The purple-white-black dress, the elegant rose in her now longer hair, the red nail polish and the matching necklace... It is all the same as the first time Izumi saw her daughter's true form, but since she is near 18 years old, she looks more mature than ever. She looks up to her mother. "Sit down and try it. Concentrate immensely and let go after it feels right in your optic nerves."

"Got it," Izumi makes a quick reply and prepares herself. She sits down and does everything she was instructed to do, but it never feels right. Every time she opens her eyes, her orbs are still baby blue.

"I did not expect you to get it right on the first try anyway," Ayame says while letting out a small sigh.

"How do you do it so effortlessly? I'm concentrating, but- "

"You're concentrating on the wrong thing," Ayame interrupts her mother. "Think of a memory that invigorates you. Something to remember for life. Something passionate."

Izumi thinks back on the life she's been living so far. One moment that she could try is the feelings she has for Yasu. She nods to the waiting daughter and sits down once again. Concentrate... and still nothing.

"Happy memories like that won't work. It must be a negative yet strong emotion," Ayame jumps in after seeing the smile on Izumi's face form during the ritual.

"But I cannot think of anything else," Izumi helplessly pleads.

"How about... your first kill? Surely, as a Behemoth, you must have killed someone or something in your life. Usually, when we take away our first life, we feel anger or remorse. Try that," Ayame says with a smug face while now crossing her arms. Whether she knows it or not, Izumi did kill once and haven't felt anything like it before. In a sick way, it was a pleasure to take his life, but she has indeed felt remorseful about it ever since.

"… Let me try, one last time," Izumi says sharply, determined to succeed this time. She concentrates of the killer feelings she had when she obliterated Ichirou's heart. Without Izumi noticing, Ayame sits down and holds her mother's hand. She feels it: She's ready now.

Concentrate, and…

… The void. A pitch-black darkness is what Izumi sees at first.

"Hello," Ayame says softly.

"Huh?! Oh, Ayame… Don't scare me like that," Izumi puts a hand on her chest to calm herself down and focus on what is in front of her. A golden key and the ancient-looking door. The two of them proceeds to the lock. Izumi takes a quick breath, unlocks it and walks in. Izumi is immediately greeted by the shadow man's red eyes, penetrating her soul. The figure is sitting on a throne she recognized from Ayame's first memories.

"Welcome, Izumi Nakashima, mother of the holy Crimson Purple princess," a dark voice is heard from the direction of the almost invisible man. Izumi is standing still in shock and fear; she didn't think she'd be so scared of him!

"It is okay, lady. You can trust me, so no need to be frightened," he says, as if reading Izumi's feelings from her aura. She now knows she cannot lie or hide anything from this man.

"Shadow man, do you have any more duties for me?", Ayame steps forward and asks. "I'm undeniably thirsty."

"Wait a little more. A princess must learn to have patience," the voice replies with a sickening tone, like that of a father scolding his child. But then, as he looks towards the scared mother, he gets an idea.

"Actually… I have a mission for the two of you, princess Ayame, mother Izumi. There is a rather common… event going on. A man groping a teenage girl in an alleyway. Locate and kill this human. This is also the time to prove yourself before you can become a member of the group, lady."

Ayame nods and is ready to leave, but her mother refuses to leave. She just looks upon the shadow with wide, lifeless eyes. "I have to… kill?"

"Yes. That shall prove your dedication to the group, but to the Crimson Purple princess as well."

She hesitates strongly on this one, but if that is what it takes to come closer to the shadow man, she might be willing to sacrifice a unworthy one. Just might. "Understood."

"Let us go now, mother. We have a job to do," Ayame says while stretching out her hand to Izumi. She accepts her hand and they fade away from the void.

The shadow man stands up and looks around with an evil look in his ruby red orbs.

"Perhaps I should have revealed a small detail to my Izumi."

The mother and daughter wake up to a cloudy evening sky, filling the room with a hue of orange. Ayame snaps her fingers and transforms into her 'hunting gear'. She goes down on one knee to tie her sneaker. "Let's hurry. I don't want to have to wait for my meal."

"Are you sure about this…?", Izumi hesitantly asks Ayame, but also herself.

"Are YOU sure about this? You're trembling an awful lot for a monster. Get your stuff together, mother. Literally," Ayame says, and with another snap, Izumi's clothes transform as well. A shade of a turquoise mask is covering her face up to her eyes, along with matching training shoes. She's wearing a black hoodie and white yoga pants with all that.

"That should do for now, I guess. I'm sorry if you don't like it, but I'm not a fashion expert," Ayame says with a smile before teleporting to her and Ayaka's bedroom window.

"Wait, Ayame! How am I supposed to follow you? I don't have your abilities; only my X-Ray vision."

"Exactly. You have your vision to help you find me. Good luck!", and out the window she jumps to start sprinting on the walls of the building like last time.

Izumi lets out a sigh and exits the apartment. She tries to be as sneaky as possible, having her purple eyes constantly activated. No one in sight can be seen. So far so good. As she gets to the elevator, Jirou Fukui, her old friend from the university years, steps out of the opening elevator doors! In the last second, Izumi manages to deactivate her eyes to greet the old-looking man.

"Why, if it isn't Izumi-chan! How are you?", Jirou cheers.

"I'm good; just going out for some jogging. Exercise has always been my strong suit, as you know!"

"I see, I see! Well, take care, Izumi-chan," Jirou says while waving goodbye, going on with his cane. Phew, that was too close of a call! If it wasn't for Jirou's unknown and strange illness that makes his body old and weak, including his eyesight, he would have spotted the dark purple laying in Izumi's. How did she not spot him in the elevator though? She dismisses the thought and figures it could be her trembling nerves.

'Taking the stairs is a far better choice, and less risky. I cannot run into more people. But, speaking of people, where is Ayame?', the worried mother thinks to herself while going down the long and cramped up stairway. When she arrives at the entrance door to the apartment complex, she decides to have a good look for Ayame before moving onward. She activates her eyes once again and finds herself travelling through the doors, the walls, the areas, until she spots Ayame at a random rooftop. She is sitting up there comfortably and patiently, with her eyes activated, just in case. Suddenly, she looks in this direction, as if she knows I'm searching for her. She stands up and waves, giving the sign that she has found the assaulter somewhere nearby. Izumi gives a firm nod before heading out in the now darker night. The only source of light is the crescent moon and some streetlights here and there. It's also a bit breezy, as Izumi's long, chestnut-colored hair dances in the air. Seems like the hectic year is finally preparing itself for autumn. Still though... who knows what more will happen? No one is expecting the Behemoth issue to simply disappear, and ironically, Izumi and Ayame are both currently part of this problem that her dear Yasu was so against. She could not feel more shame in her heart, but she has no choice at this point. Do or die.

She uses her superhuman speed to keep Ayame from waiting.

"I've been waiting for a moment like this, hunting with my mother, yet you make me wait?", Ayame makes a slight complain.

"Do you constantly forget that we're not the same in rank? Stop complaining and just lead me through it."

"Look over there, at the bar. I've been observing the people inside, and all are men except the teenage girl. It feels strange though... She's drinking with them, all smile and laughter. It's most likely an act so she can get away when she finds a chance."

"So...?"

"So, the plan is to go in and kill every one of them. Except the teenager, of course."

"That's the plan?! Just go in and kill everybody in the bar?!", Izumi shockingly exclaims how her daughter could be so cold.

"I helped you; now you help me," Ayame says in a voice of anger.

"… Fine. One final question: How do I… you know… kill?"

"Everyone has their own way of killing. Since you're a mutated Behemoth, you probably won't fancy the taste of blood, so be creative and finish the job in a way that fits you. As long as it gets done, I'll be satisfied." And with those words, Ayame jumps down from the roof and onto the hard ground, with Izumi following her lead.

"Wait," Ayame suddenly whispers out and pushes herself and her mother behind a corner. They watch from their hiding spot as the intoxicated teenager stumbles out of the bar with the helping shoulder of what looks like the bartender. He has monotone-colored clothing, consisting of a white shirt with a black vest on top of it, along with matching trousers going all the way down to his shoes. However, they cannot see his face or hear his voice, since he's turned away and silent as a mouse, but he's quite tall and slender. They continue out of the alleyway and across the street, where a convenient motel has taken place.

"Mother."

Izumi immediately activates her X-Ray eyes to document what's going on inside. "The bartender booked a room for them until morning. They go upstairs to room 207."

"Let's hurry before we run out of time. Take my hand; we're teleporting."

"Huh- Okay…?", Izumi quizzingly says while taking hold of Ayame's hand. In a split second, they are at the motel's entrance.

"Don't just stand there! Let's move!", Ayame snaps Izumi out of the dizziness from the teleportation and they go inside. Luckily enough, there is no one at the reception now, so they use their superhuman speed to quickly enough find room 207.

"Ready?", Ayame asks with hunger in her voice.

"Ready," Izumi confirms.

Ayame kicks open the door with an incredible strength in her left foot. Inside, they find something unexpected. The girl is laying dead on the bed while the man is kneeling politely with his head down as soon as

Ayame goes in. She checks his aura right away with the help of her powers. "He is a Behemoth."

"Really? Why doesn't he speak up then?", Izumi asks, looking at Ayame first and then down at the mysterious bartender... until he opens his mouth.

"How about I simply look up at you, little Izumi?"

"How do you know my name?", she makes a threatening remark in her question.

"Oh, I know much more about you than you think. But the fact that you don't recognize my voice does make me a bit sad... My Izumi."

"'My Izumi'? No... Are you...

... Ichirou Fukui?!"

"What if I am? Are you going to run up and hug me, dear?", the mysterious man asks in a seductive evil. He has the appearance, the voice, the personality, and calls Izumi his. There is no doubt in her mind: This is Ichirou, in the flesh.

"How are you alive?! I... I...!"

"You killed me? Ah, yes, you did. Almost." He licks his lips with an unusually long tongue while saying this. It's more than disturbing.

"Well, if you aren't dead yet... I'll finish you off again!", Izumi says while bursting forward and using all her abilities to crush this man's heart. But after crushing it to bits and pieces, his appearance changes drastically. He's transforming into someone very familiar. An old-looking man with a cane.

"Izumi-chan... Why did you fall for it...?", are Jirou's last words before he slowly falls to the carpet floor, dead as a fly.

"Wow. I didn't think you'd be able to kill the old filthy rapist, mother," Ayame casually says. Izumi stands in shock though. No words are escaping her mouth. Did she just brutally kill her closest friend because he looked too much like Ichirou? Was it all an illusion to deceive her? Is she going mad? As she is not responding at all to her daughter, Ayame lets out a casual sigh and goes to the body to drink the little lively blood it has. But Izumi stops her by forcefully grabbing her arm.

"DON'T. TOUCH. HIM." Her eyes are gleaming with the purpleness and the teeth as of a wild animal are back. She really is threatening her daughter. Ayame becomes confused by her mother's reaction.

"What's wrong, mother? Do you want his blood? If you do, go ahead. You were the one who killed him, after a- "

"SHUT UP!", Izumi makes another threat while the small horns are growing. She is, once more, unconsciously letting her negative emotions take over, revealing everything in both actions and words.

"IT WAS ALL FAKE!"

"What was fake...?"

"JIROU DID NOT DESERVE TO BECOME A PAWN BY ICHIROU!"

"Jirou? Ichirou? Who are you talking about?", Ayame asks without really expecting a response at this point. 'Maybe the killing was too much for her...', Ayame tries to come up with a conclusion in her mind. "You're clearly upset for some reason, so I'll wait outside for a bit, mother," Ayame says without a spark in her voice. As she heads down the stairs and to the main lobby, she hears Izumi's traumatizing screams echo in the halls. The receptionist is there, and Ayame lays down a few coins, saying "Keep the change" before heading out with hands in her pockets. After a while of screaming, Izumi gradually goes back to her normal appearance. She begins talking to the man in question, hoping he's listening, somehow, somewhere.

"Ichirou... I'll make sure that, next time I see you, I'll slay your heart, once and for all. I'll punch your guts out. I'll gouge your eyes out. This means war, Ichirou. War." And, as if her prayers have been heard, the void is temporarily filling a furious Izumi up, just for the shadow man to show himself. It looks like the two are having a glaring competition, the dark purple versus the ruby red.

"So, you did figure me out. From the very beginning as well, it seems like. I'm not surprised though, as I know my Izumi is a very intelligent woman."

"Show yourself, vermin. I want to see you in physical form so I can tear you apart," Izumi demands.

"Oh? Have you missed me? Or perhaps you've had a change of heart after I killed off Yasu, used Jirou as a pawn and raped your beautiful Behemoth girl, princess Ayame?"

"What… What in the world are you saying…?"

"You heard me. The young princess and I have been one. Her 12-year-old protesting screams were oh, so wonderful. How she wanted to be 'like everyone else'. Like mother, like daughter. What is more amusing is that she does not remember any of it!"

Izumi is slowly going back to the state she originally was in before calming herself down. Her voice is going from sweet and melodious to raw and vicious, her humane teeth are changing themselves into canine teeth, and she has her small horns sticking out slightly above her forehead. The more she transforms, the louder growling can be heard from her.

"I'm honored to see your true form, my Izumi. You look stunning, but it's nothing compared to little Ayame. When she gets mad, I can merely envision how she'll glow behind those powers in her eyes. She did activate her abilities after I took her virginity, after all. A 'thank you' would never hurt."

"YOU DISGUST ME!", she says with a dangerous and powerful roar.

"To be frank, I don't care what you think of me, ma chérie. At least not anymore. Your daughter, however…", he hints what he wants to express in his eyes. They're looking at Izumi flirtatiously, as if that's the only thing he desires in the world. Power, lust and blood. "Speaking of her, she is waiting for you, no? You may go. Oh, by the way; she won't believe you if you tell her the truth. For Ayame, the world is the perpetrator, and I am salvation," is the last thing Ichirou says before fading away into the darkness of the void, leaving a speechless Izumi in reality. She can barely breathe, grasping for air between her sudden, violent sobs. One final shriek of complete terror and trauma lets out from the very depths of her soul, until she decides to get her messed up self together and go away from this sleazy motel.

"Took you long enough. Have you calmed down?", Izumi is greeted by these words and a smiling Ayame who is having her natural blue orbs locked on the crescent-shaped moon. Izumi looks like she hasn't slept for days, which Ayame notices. "Did you cry that much over a kill?"

"I have to tell you something, Ayame, but let's go over it when we're home. It's a long story... I just want to feel safe right now, which I don't, at the moment," Izumi lazily says and begins to walk a slow stroll all the way to their apartment complex building, which can be seen in the distance. Ayame sees clearly that her mother needs support, so she walks beside her, in Izumi's own, painful pace.

They arrive home, and Izumi is still in a catatonic state, physically and mentally. All she needs right now is a good night's sleep, so when they walk into the family apartment, she passes out on her futon as soon as she enters the master bedroom. Ayame is deeply worried for her mother's health and begins wondering if taking her on a hunting session was a good idea. Obviously, something else happened that Ayame knows she is not aware of yet, so she settles herself to talk with the shadow man while the exhausted mother sleeps peacefully.

After effortlessly performing the ritual, she enters the void, goes into the sanctuary and sees the blurry figure sitting at a table with his intertwined hands holding up his chin. He seems to be thinking deeply, until he notices Ayame.

"Ah, welcome back, Crimson Purple. How did the mission with Izumi go? Did you fulfill it?"

"She passed the test, but something is bothering me. Anyhow, why did you send us to kill a Behemoth, one of our kind?"

"Behemoth or not, a sexual assaulter will always be one in the end. You know I would never deceive a good young woman like you, do you not?"

He comes off as suspicious to Ayame, but the princess plays along so she doesn't raise her own meter. Besides, why doubt a man who has helped her with finding a decent purpose in life? But that is kind of off in the first place. Why did he indeed help her come this far? What does he gain from it? Ayame starts to question it more and more.

"Whatever you say, shadow man. I'm going back now. Until then..."

Leaving a disguised Ichirou in thought, he decides to take a glass of blood-red wine and relax at the dinner table. "So, Ayame does suspect me… Perhaps I shouldn't have been too cocky for my own good. It was a big enough risk killing off Jirou as such, but oh well… That pathetic excuse of a Behemoth needed to die. Let us see…- "He takes a big clunk of the drink and continues talking to himself, finishing his sentence. "Let us see how this war turns out, my feisty Izumi." With a snap of his fingers, he summons the members of the group. Everyone is sitting at their respective seats at the long table.

"Why did you summon us, master?", one man speaks up behind his masquerade mask.

"We have traitors among us: The holy Crimson Purple princess and her mother, Izumi Nakashima. Thus, from tomorrow, it is time for them to pay the price with blood. You all know whose blood, don't you?"

"… Humans," another one with a feminine voice answer.

"Correct. Even innocent ones are our foes. Go now; prepare for tomorrow's biggest hunt of Behemoth history!", the shadow man says with a courageous and determined voice, with a hint of evilness in it, of course. With that small speech finished, everyone fades away from view. 'I'm going to win,' he thinks to himself while a wide, dark smile is displaying itself on his pale face, now stained with red from the wine.

Ayame wakes up on the floor in her bedroom. After seeing how bewildered her mother became during the hunt, someone who is usually cool-headed, she is beginning to wonder, 'who is really the righteous one in this world?'. She changes clothes to her pajamas and lays in her bed, one question after the other popping up in her head and heart. 'I just want Behemoths and humanity to live in harmony and equality…', the young woman has this one last, sad thought before falling asleep. The mother and daughter sleep soundly through the remaining night and the sunrise, until their sleep is disturbed by a loud and obnoxious knocking on the front door. Ayame and Izumi quickly exit their rooms, looks at one another and nods. Who knows if this is an attack or not? Izumi proceeds to go to the locked door, ready to activate her pair of powers at any moment. When she unlocks it, she is immediately being jumped on… by Sora. "We're hoooome!", Ayaka and Sora exclaims happily, with their arms outstretched in the air.

"You woke us up, Ayaka," Ayame makes a complain. "Look how tired we are."

"Sorry, sorry! We forgot the keys on the kitchen counter when we were going to leave, so we had no choice."

"Why are you home already, anyways? The trip was supposed to go on for a week, no?"

"They had to cancel the remaining things of the trip because of the awful weather that suddenly struck. It's terrible outside! Have you seen it?"

Ayame and Izumi listens to Ayaka and goes to the window. It's a strange storm going on, like a blizzard but without the snow. It's hard to see out. The wind is picking up immensely, blowing smaller objects from the streets as if cleaning it. There are also small raindrops on the window, and that's when they both notice how wet these two explorers are from the rain that felt like joining the storm.

"My dears, you must be freezing! I'll get some towels and make tea," Izumi says while hastily going to the kitchen. She gets a type of déjà vu from this: The day Yasu and Reina died. But she cannot let their deaths bother her this much. She needs to think about the present and the remaining people in this life that she cares about. Of course, she cannot stop thinking about Ichirou and the things he has said and done. Izumi must admit that she did not understand everything he told her in the void at the motel, but somehow, he was behind Yasu's death as well as Jirou's. Not to mention the horrible trauma he has set upon Ayame… At only the age of 12 too… As she is waiting for the tea and goes to get the towels and new clothes for Ayaka and Sora, she looks at every one of her children with sad eyes. Isn't a mother supposed to protect her children from harm and give them hope? Izumi feels completely embarrassed to call herself a mother. She feels as if she has failed that role miserably. She decides that, from now on, she won't disappoint her children ever again.

"Here, children. Fresh clothes and fluffy towels are in the bathroom. Get inside and change," Izumi smiles with her teeth showing. What she doesn't realize is that her mental state hasn't fully recovered, and she still has small but longer teeth.

"Uhm, mother... Are you okay? Your teeth...", Ayaka says puzzled while pointing at Izumi's mouth. The mother realizes that she almost revealed her true self. "Oh! No, I just smiled too hard, haha!", Izumi says while thinking to herself how bad of a liar she is, but the lie should work on these two.

"Oh. Whatever; we're going to the bathroom to wash up now! Come on, Sora!", Ayaka shrugs it off, Sora takes her hand, and they go change. After they're gone, Ayame lays down her book, gets up from the sofa and looks at her mother. "You almost showed Ayaka what we are. Be careful," Ayame says as if it's an order which it technically is.

"Sorry, Ayame... I'll be cautious from now on. By the way... can we talk in my room while they're in the bathroom? Let's keep our voices down and we should be fine." Izumi wants to ignore Ichirou's words and believe I Ayame and that she'll trust her mother over a perpetrator.

"Fine by me," Ayame accepts, and they head off to sit at a small kotatsu table in the master bedroom. "So, what do you want to talk about?"

"I don't know where to start, dear."

"Start from the beginning."

Izumi takes a deep breath and tells Ayame everything, from start to finish. She tells her about her times in university and how she got to know Yasu, Ichirou & Jirou Fukui, what happened between her and Jirou at the motel and so on.

"Okay... But what has this to do with me?", Ayame asks.

"I don't know how to say this without it coming as a shock for you, but... Ichirou, the Behemoth who raped me, is two things: The shadow man, and your rapist as well. He is the one behind everything, including killing your father and his twin brother, Jirou."

Ayame's blue irises are wide open, staring right at her mother. She cannot believe what Izumi has told her up until now. It all adds up, but she refuses to believe the story about the shadow man's true identity.

"You're not... serious... are you?"

"Can't you tell I'm dead serious, Ayame?"

"But- "

"There is no 'but'. I swear on your and my own life that this information are all facts. Please… you must trust me over Ichirou. He's pure evil and is manipulating you and your powers for some sinful reason. I don't know why yet, but let's figure it out togeth- "

"And why should I believe you?", Ayame coldly asks, interrupting her mother. The question sounds more like a statement though, like she already decided she won't believe Izumi.

"Who am I to you, Ayame? I am your mother. On the other hand, who is the shadow man to you?"

"He is my savior. He taught me everything about surviving in this world as a Behemoth, which you never even noticed that I was. He also gave me a purpose, and that is saving victims of sexual assaults."

"Do you feel content with doing whatever he tells you, obeying him like a puppy? You're the reincarnation of Crimson Purple, a legend amongst us, and you decide this slavery and killings should continue? Yes, I know I made the grave mistake of not recognizing your nature, and I will regret it for the rest of my life, but you need to understand! I don't mean you any harm, while Ichirou, our rapist, does!", Izumi's words are hastily being thrown out. She wishes her daughter hears her desperate plea. However, Ayame is silent. All she's doing is looking down at her slightly shaking legs. It seems like she doesn't have any arguments left: That, or she is trying to come up with arguments that'll leave Izumi speechless.

"I love you," the emotional mother tells her dear child. Looking outside the window, she continues, "I'm sure this storm is bad news from Ichirou. I declared war against him, so he must be preparing. I know; it was selfish of me to danger human and Behemoth lives, both the guilty and the innocent. What was I supposed to do though? He's clearly a threat to all creatures in this world."

"War…?", Ayame says out loud. It seems like she is still determining whose side to be on. It could indeed all be true, and to find that out, she decides to walk up to Izumi and lay her slender hand on top of the mother's forehead.

"Ayame? What are you- ", and suddenly, Izumi notices how someone has entered her mind. A beautiful girl with crimson and purple eyes. It sure does seem like Ayame is striving towards believing her mother; all she needs now is proof. Ayame concentrates, searching through every recent memory until she, quickly enough, finds the memories from the motel hunting session. She watches the whole thing and, yes, it all makes sense now. She has the proof and the trusting words of a loving mother. At this point, she cannot ask for more.

Ayame lets go of Izumi's head and looks at her. "I believe you, after seeing everything you've experienced with the shadow... no, with Ichirou Fukui." She looks at her hands as if they're covered in dirt and smiles sadly. "How could I have been so fooled... all this time..." Eventually, a small, solitary teardrop falls onto her palm, laying there in a sparkling circle. "I don't want to believe what I now know, but I don't have time to be in denial. I must trust myself. I just... feel nothing but stupid at this point." The more Ayame talks, the more wet her hands become from the silent drops trickling their way down. She is not even mad at Ichirou right now. She's just mad at herself for being ignorant enough to be manipulated by a serial rapist, those she has sworn to kill, for six whole years. An interrupting voice stops Ayame's thoughts.

"I can't imagine everything you two have been through, and I'm sorry you had to face it all by yourselves, but we're here."

"What do you mean, mother?", Ayame, with head buried in her knuckles, exclaims. But Izumi's response is quiet. She's only staring at one direction with her mouth hanging, and that is the opened door where Ayaka and Sora is standing. They have been there the whole time, hearing every single word and witnessing every single action.

"Ayaka, Sora!?", the gasping mother and sentimental daughter say at the same time.

"Doesn't big sis have beautiful eyes, Sora?", Ayaka shows her genuine smile and picks up Sora so he can see the red and the purple in Ayame's teary orbs.

"Yes! I love you, big sister!", Sora says while hugging Ayame. She fills up with true love and trust, making her negative emotions disappear as quickly as they arrived. She sniffs a bit, wipes her eyes and looks at little Sora, saying "Well, you have big, beautiful eyes too, Sora" to the happy boy. That natural happiness that he was born with makes even Ayame smile. However, Izumi is slightly freaking out in the background.

"Gosh, what are we going to do now that you know our secret…?!", she makes a panicked remark. "Please, you have to understand us! We never wanted this!" But she is interrupted by Ayame.

"Stop, mother. There is no use getting hysteric now. Besides, I've already checked their auras; they don't have any ill feelings towards you nor me. That's why I'm welcoming them with open arms."

"I've always known that you're a Behemoth, Ayame. Same with you, mother. You are my twin, and you are my mother, so how could I not have noticed it? I would've been the foolish one if I didn't even recognize my own family." She sets Sora down to walk around on his own while she continues speaking. "Despite being a human, I'm not afraid of the two of you. I have no reason to be, either." Izumi must admit that she is a bit shocked, hearing her sweet Ayaka tell them that she doesn't hold a grudge towards neither one. She really is too carefree for her own good, but at the same time, both Izumi and Ayame are relieved to hear this.

"Are you not confused, Ayaka? You just heard and saw us admit to our abilities, yet there's so much you don't know," Ayame curiously asks.

"Of course, I am! I don't even know what to say or do anymore myself, but what I do know is that I'll be there for all of you. Including when you're killing that rapist," Ayaka exclaims confidently.

"Who said we're going to kill him?"

"It's written all over your face. You're going to save the world or something, right? So, do it. Do it as soon as possible, because, like mother said, this snow-free blizzard is bad news."

"Very well. I'll fill you in on the details, because you need to know everything if you're going with us," Ayame says while preparing the ritual to the void, but she stops. She is sensing numerous people outside, and almost all of them have terrifying auras. She alarms Izumi to immediately activate her X-Ray vision and look around for suspicious people. After a second, just a second, she gasps as she is running to the window.

"What is it, mother? Inform me."

"Ichirou isn't planning on starting the war in the void. He's already started in reality… this world. Look outside."

The twins make their way to their mother's side, and as soon as they look out the window, they are greeted with a view beyond horrible: Humans are, without success, running for their lives as Behemoths everywhere are staining the streets with so much blood that the crying sky cannot even wipe the grounds clean. Thunder and lightning bolts down, some hitting innocent people unusually close. It's so intense that it feels like an earthquake joined the disasters too.

Wait...

"Ayaka, Ayame, Sora; get down!", Izumi screams out of nowhere, as the ground starts shaking furiously. The lights in the house go out and all that is seen is Izumi's and Ayame's glowing eyes. Books and other miscellaneous items are heard falling from the shelf in the living room.

Suddenly, it's pitch silent, and the earthquake subsided for now. Everyone sits in the darkness, worried about what else could happen.

"Ayame?", Izumi asks, searching for her daughter.

"I'm here. Do you have a plan?"

"Only for this moment: Let us travel to the void. It's a fabricated space for Ichirou, after all. We should be fine there."

"Going towards Ichirou is a suicide mission. You are not aware of how powerful he is. I wouldn't recommend it."

"Do you have a better idea? He needs to die anyways, and I know how to kill him!"

"You don't know anything. You failed in the past because you don't know the real way of killing a Behemoth of his and my rank."

"How do you do it then?"

"You must kill yourself willingly. You need to make sure that you have no lust for life in your mind, heart or soul in order for it to work. There is another way, but..."

"I suppose this Ichirou will be almost impossible to kill, if that's the case...", Ayaka jumps into the conversation and lets out a disappointing sigh. "I think we should give it a try anyway!"

Ayame and Izumi both nod in the dark and decides to carefully prepare the ritual for going to the void, taking Ayaka and Sora with them. What awaits them there, well...

CHAPTER V

The twins, the little brother and the mother are all in the void. Ayame is the only one with the golden key for the giant door. "It seems like he's only expecting to see me," she proclaims. Ayaka takes a hold of her sister's left hand. "No, we are going in this together." They all take a deep breath as Ayame slowly opens the old door to what is going to be a battle between life, death and afterlife.

The shadow man is the first thing they see in the throne of the long main hall. He gets excited when he sees the four of them all barging into his space.

"Oho, what is this? A family meeting?", he lets out some sarcasm while sitting in an all too comfortable position. He takes a sip of some white wine beside him. "Ugh, this tastes disgusting. Would you like some, Ayame?"

"Ichirou Fukui...!", Ayame exclaims in a raw tone. Just the mere sight of him gets her blood boiling, to the point where she is forming herself into the truest nature she can form into. Long, gray horns are growing out of her forehead, her teeth become monster-like, and on top of that, she's transfiguring into her traditional attire, turning her into the Crimson Purple princess that she's been hiding within. The air feels extraordinary because of her intense aura engulfing it.

"I suppose you don't drink yet, young lady," the man says while smashing the wine glass onto the floor and changing into his physical form like it's nothing, and it is a hideous sight. His skin has turned misty black, his white horns are frightening, and his smile is vicious beyond belief.

"Well then... Let us begin, Ayame."

Ayame snaps with her fingers to spawn a weapon in her hand: a light brown staff with a yellow spark of luminance emitting from the top. "Ah, so we're having this kind of battle, are we? I shall pick out my own weapon of choice then!", Ichirou says with a now much darker tone to his voice, while a strange yet beautiful dagger is appearing instantly in his right hand. Ayame wonders why he would choose something so small as a dagger from his weaponry, but then she realizes it is Azrael's Blade, a mythical blade of Death that can easily kill anyone who gets touched by it, including the most powerful Behemoth alive. That was the other way of killing a Behemoth that Ayame never mentioned to the rest of them.

"Azrael's Blade... I have been in the afterlife once, after all, thanks to Izumi. I simply decided to take a souvenir with me. This fight should be over rather quickly now," Ichirou casually threatens Ayame.

"I'm going to kill you so fast that you won't even be able to return it!", Ayame screams back while shooting different types of balls of powers from the mystical staff, everything from acid and ice to fire and lava. He dodges every single attack from Ayame with ease, as if he's dancing with the blade, waiting for the best opportunity to strike. She notices his tactic and begins running up the walls with her superhuman speed, occasionally teleporting to dodge his lethal attacks. He laughs maniacally while stabbing the air, trying to desperately hit Crimson Purple. She needs to recharge eventually, so she keeps her cool and uses her specialty and her own individual power: Invisibility.

"This isn't fun at all, Ayame! Amuse me more!", a disappointed Ichirou complains with a sinister smile placed on his face. He lays his focus on his optic nerves and lets his ruby red eyes take control of trying to find her well-hidden aura. He grows more and more frustrated, as he looks around and no princess is to be found.

"Come out! I order you!", Ichirou says while his ears and eyes are starting to deform as well. They're getting slightly bigger and more in the shape of an oval. It looks like they will pop out of his eye sockets at any given moment. During his deformation, Ayame takes this opportunity to launch another attack with her staff. Acid begins pouring into his eyes. "AHHH! IT HURTS! Damn you, Ayame..."

He did this on purpose however, to make his senses more attuned.

After checking the ceiling, he feels a slight aura from the gigantic chandelier positioned behind him.
"FOUND YOU!", Ichirou stabs the air where he feels the sensation.
It was a miss. He stabbed the mere aura of Ayame, but not her. She's hiding elsewhere, and little does he know that she's now visible behind him. "You don't order me anymore," she says while, in the blink of an eye, taking Azrael's Blade from Ichirou's deformed hands. Clumsily enough, he actually fell for it, and Ayame now has the Blade of Death in her possession. It's unusually heavy though; she can barely hold it, and therefore drops it. Both Ayame and Ichirou take this chance to use their immense speed to get down to the floor and grab the small blade.
Before either one of them gets there, Ayaka had sneaked out of Izumi's, Sora's and her hiding spot in the void to try to help her sister. When she walks into the hall and sees nothing but flashes and an interesting dagger on the ground, she runs quickly to the blade's side, gets it and uses all her strength to push it right above her head, where Ichirou is coming from. She hopes she can hit him, considering the state of his scarred eyes. A roar of determination is let out as she's wielding it.
However, Ichirou sees all of this and uses this moment to slip in and try to grab the knife and push it right through the body of the bothersome hindrance.
"AYAKA!", Izumi screams while using her superhuman speed in the last second to take Ayaka's place. Time stops for what feels like an eternity. Izumi only needed one quick blow and that took her life, sacrificing herself to push Ayaka away, saving her daughter.
The mother's lifeless body falls to the floor like a doll. It happened so fast that barely Ayame, yet alone Ayaka, was able to see what occurred. But they both did indeed see it. The death of Izumi Nakashima. Ichirou, who's now holding a bloody blade, puts up an ironic smile.
"My, my... The whore did something good for once? I'm surprised but disappointed. I didn't want to kill her like this. Oh well." He turns his gaze towards the shocked Ayaka. "And you, girlie? You're going to join your mother as soon as I'm finished with your siste- "

Ichirou starts to suddenly cough up black blood. 'What's happening?' He looks around but there's no one here. Ayaka is gone too. From nowhere, his vision becomes pure white. Nothing can be seen or heard except his own thoughts. His memory becomes blurrier by the minute, strangely.
'What was I just doing? I can't remember.'
'How can someone like me live?'
'Actually… who am I?'

"Found you," Ayame says to herself while slowly letting go of the dimmed Ichirou's back. She holds up her staff, making it disappear into thin air, now that her duty is complete, and the world's threat is gone. Ayaka, who is still startled but can talk, asks, "What did you do to him? He is completely frozen right now."
"I erased all his memories. Well, except the ones where he feels miserable about himself. Even evil like him can feel these types of things."
"Oh…", Ayaka says, letting a gaze slip to their mother's body. "She's gone, isn't she…?"
"… Yeah. But she's in a good place now. A peaceful place where father and Reina were waiting for her."
"I hope so."
"Let's continue living on. For their sakes," Ayame says while taking Azrael's Blade, positioning it towards Ichirou's heart and making him hold it. His dull eyes look down at the blade for a minute and, with no hesitation, he turns it the other way and forces it into Ayame's heart.
"I GOT YOU, WITH THE LAST OF MY POWER!", are his last words before he pulls out the dagger from Ayame's chest and stabs himself to death, making him truly dead this time.
"AYAME!", Ayaka lets out a startled shriek and crawls over to her twin sister. She's still breathing. "Oh my gosh, you're alive!" But just as she says so, Ayame's breathing becomes less and less.
"Ayame…? Wake up! Please," Ayaka is begging while sobbing down at the hands she's holding: she's holding Ayame's and Izumi's cold, deceased hands.

Suddenly, Ayaka and a passed-out Sora are being transferred into reality. Everything is as normal again outside. No people though, as if the country had been wiped out. But it's peaceful... for her grief.

Azrael's Blade followed her too. She picks it up. "What should I do now...?", talking with herself as she's holding the blade, thinking about finishing everything. But just as she's going to, she hears a voice from somewhere. It's like a soft, friendly echo.

"Continue living on. For our sakes," a transparent Ayame in white cloth is appearing before Ayaka, telling her this.

"But... without you... what am I going to do? Everyone and everything is gone. I have nothing."

"You're awfully pessimistic for having such a carefree personality, sister," Ayame says while smiling. She soon starts to fade away though. "Oh, looks like it's already my time to go. But don't worry, Ayaka! I died happily, fulfilling my mission in life as the Crimson Purple princess."

"Will I ever see you again, Ayame?"
"I don't know, Ayaka...

How tightly can you close your eyes?"